WOK AROUND ASIA
ORIENTAL FLAVORS COOKED IN A WOK

Other books by Yukiko Moriyama-Trunnell:

Tofu Cook Book (1982, now in its 9th printing)

Sushi Cook Book (1983, 13th printing 1993), co-authored with a sushi chef

Japanese Cuisine for Everyone (1984, 13th printing 1993)

Korean Cooking for Everyone (1986, 3rd printing 1992), co-authored with a Korean chef

Favorite Japanese Dishes (1987, 3rd printing 1991)

A Taste of Tofu (1988, 3rd printing 1993)

Chicken Cookbook (1990, 2nd printing 1993)

Japanese Snacks & Light Meals (1991, reprinted 1992)

Sandwich Cookbook (1992), co-authored with a sandwich shop owner in Florida.

Note: All books are published in both Japanese and English. The Sushi Cook Book is also available in a Spanish version.

PUBLISHER REPRESENTATIVE OFFICE

UNITED STATES: Prime Communication System
P.O. BOX 456 Shaw Island, WA 98286

AUTHOR'S SALES AGENCY: A. K. HARANO COMPANY
P.O. BOX 1022 Edmonds, WA 98020
Phone: (206) 774-5490 Fax: (206) 774-5490
D & BH ENTERPRISES
94-443 Kahuanani Street, Waipahu, HI 96797
Phone: (808) 671-6041

OVERSEAS DISTRIBUTORS

UNITED STATES: JP TRADING, INC.
300 Industrial Way
Brisbane, Calif. 94005
Phone: (415) 468-0775, 0776 Fax: (415) 469-8038

MEXICO: Publicaciones Sayrols, S.A. de C. V.

COLOMBIA: Jorge E. Morales & CIA. LTDA.

TAIWAN: Formosan Magazine Press, Ltd.

HONG KONG: Apollo Book Company, Ltd.

THAILAND: Central Department Store Ltd.

SINGAPORE: MPH DISTRIBUTORS (S) PTE, LTD.

MALAYSIA: MPH DISTRIBUTORS SDN, BHD.

PHILIPPINES: National Book Store, Inc.

KOREA: Tongjin Chulpan Muyeok Co., Ltd.

INDONESIA: C.V. TOKO BUKU "MENTENG"

INDIA: Dani Book Land, Bombay 14

AUSTRALIA: BOOKWISE INTERNATIONAL

GUAM, SIPAN AND MICRONESIAN ISLANDS: FUJIWARA'S SALES & SERVICE

CANADA: MILESTONE PUBLICATIONS

U.S.A: MASA T. & ASSOCIATES

ISBN4-915831-44-2

ACKNOWLEDGEMENTS

I wish to express my heartfelt gratitude to many people far and near for their invaluable assistance in the making of "WOK AROUND ASIA-ORIENTAL FLAVORS COOKED IN A WOK".

First I would like to acknowledge and give warm thanks to my publisher, Shiro Shimura, for his trust and faith in my work; to editor in chief, Akira Naito, who kindled my enthusiasm and got the project going.

I would also like to acknowledge and give special warm thanks for the contributions made by friends: Masao Tokuyama, whose photographic talents are readily evident as being of the highest caliber; Koji Abe, whose editorial assistance was indispensable...... his hard work and dedication are much appreciated, and have keys to the success of my projects; Naoko Ito, whose patience and sense of design are much appreciated; Noriko Komatsu, my thanks for her secretarial help; Harriet Kofalk, whose professional writing ability was indispensable for making English language complexities simple; Katsuko Ueno of Spice House for the test supplies of spices and herbs; Yukiko Hasegawa, who introduced me to special Ponape Kuching black and white peppers from Ponpei Island, Federated States of Micronesia; Chizuko Ogata, who lent me magnificent dishes; Murasaki Fukue Kô Minagawa for her illustrations; and finally Eiko Ohishi, whose hard work and help in the kitchen are always greatly appreciated.

I am indebted to you all for your support, encouragement and patience during the many months of writing.

INTRODUCTION

Customs and traditions of more countries reach us today through travel, advanced communication and contacts of many kinds. Food customs and traditions are an important part of these connections. We may find that we like a curry-based dish we discover in Malaysia, a soy-flavored soup from Japan or China, and a coconut-milk-based dish from Thailand. As we experiment with new combinations in other aspects of our lives, why not experiment with combining foods from many lands?

This book is an introduction to Asian flavors from many countries. It is based on my personal experience of traveling throughout the Orient and cooking the dishes of each country I visit. Eleven years ago, when I published my first cookbook. *Quick and Easy Tofu Cook Book*, I was pleased to bring readers the benefits of a diet which included ways to use tofu in many different recipes. Since then I have published nine other cookbooks, each of them contributing to the experinece I bring you in this one.

We are more experimental today both in our tastes and in the combinations of foods we appreciate. A new generation of gourmets takes pride and pleasure in preparing these foods, but you need not be a gourmet to do so. Many people have also become more aware of the importance of good nutrition, and we can all improve our health through preparing our own foods. The quick-cooking techniques for using a wok provide still another way to enjoy these delicious combinations.

Whether you combine recipes from Japan, China and Thailand to create a feast, or choose to serve a meal from any one of those origins, you will find that the recipes in this book are easy to cook and take only a short time to prepare. Special ingredients called for are generally available in natural food stores, in the gourmet sections of supermarkets, or in Oriental food markets. They are simply another part of the experiment-and the satisfaction-of sharing other cultures.

It is my pleasure to share these quick and delicious recipes with you. So heat up your wok to embark on Oriental cuisine, and enjoy the good nutrition that comes with it.

Yukiko Moriyama-Trunnell
Tokyo, Japan
August, 1993

BASIC TIPS

MENU PLANNING

1. SEASONAL APPROPRIATENESS

Special attention should be given to the ingredients you choose. Some fresh fish and vegetables are available only at certain times of the year. Therefore, consider using seasonal ingredients which are abundant in the market.

2. OCCASION

Consider the number of people you serve and whether you serve for a festive occasion, luncheon, dinner or picnic, etc.

3. FLAVOR AND TEXTURE

Plan your menu with meat, fish and vegetables. Make each dish with a different cooking method such as stir-fried, steamed, fried, etc.

4. COLOR

Presentation of food is also important. Each ingredients has a different flavor, texture and color. It is important to appeal to the eye as well as to the tongue.

5. NUTRITION

It helps when determining the kind of food to serve to find out the diner's physical condition and age.

6. COST

Seasonal fresh items generally have lower prices. See the weekly special for your menu planning.

BEFORE YOU BEGIN

These basic tips will save you time and make for the successful preparation of WOK COOKING.

STEP I

1. Read recipes carefully and thoroughly, paying special attention to The Cornstarch for Thickening section appearing in the Stir-Frying section. Become acquainted with the techniques of cooking and the various equipment available to accomplish this purpose. Always read the entire recipe before you attempt to cook.

2. Write down all necessary ingredients you need to buy.

3. Check all cooking equipment and place within reach.

4. Arrange all necessary seasonings, spices and herbs on the kitchen counter or within your reach. Recipes calling for *mirin*, a Japanese sweet cooking wine, should not be replaced with Chinese wine. Chinese rice wine and *mirin* are not directly interchangeable. Soup stock may be used in recipes. This will result in a richer flavor. Canned chicken broth is a good substitute if you do not have time to make your own.

The use of garlic enhances the flavor of cooked food. Crushed or minced garlic may be added to almost any dishes. Just add the crushed or minced garlic to oil heating in the wok. After the flavor has been released, the garlic may be removed or left in the wok while cooking the rest of the ingredients. Also, the use of grated fresh ginger root enhances the flavor of cooked food.

The recipes contained in this book were tested and developed using Japanese soy sauce which is considered a medium soy sauce. Use a medium soy sauce unless otherwise specified for the best results. *Sake*, Japanese rice wine and Shaohsing, Chinese rice wine may be replaced with dry sherry in most recipes. Slicing meat against the grain of the long muscle fibers will result in added tenderness when the meat is cooked. Partially-frozen meat is easier to slice and more uniform slices can be obtained.

5. Prepare measuring cups and spoons.

6. Place all serving bowls, plates and platters near you. You may need to keep some serving platters warm.

STEP II

1. Put comfortable clothes on and wear an apron, so that you will be psychologically ready for cooking.

2. Prepare plenty of kitchen towels and paper towels on hand.

STEP III

Hot food should be placed on a warmed plate and cold food on a chilled plate. Also look at the design on the plate, if any, before you place food on it. Place the plate so that the design faces the diner. With a towel, wipe off around the rim if there are spilled bits or traces of liquid.

STEP IV

Always use your judgement in the substitution of ingredients called for in a recipe. Most ingredients used in this book are explained in the ingredients section. Be creative and do not be afraid to adapt the recipes to your own personal taste.

CONTENTS

ACKNOWLEDGEMENTS ···3

INTRODUCTION ··4

BASIC TIPS & BEFORE YOU BEGIN ······················5

METRIC TABLES · BASIC COOKING INFORMATION ·····8

GETTING TO KNOW YOUR WOK ·······················9

UTENSILS ··10
SEASONING YOUR WOK ····································11

STIR-FRYING, SAUTÉING ··································12

SHRIMP WITH VEGETABLES ······························13
EGG FU YUNG ···14
SWEET & SOUR PORK ··15
SEAFOOD FRIED RICE · FRIED RICE ··········16 · 17
CHINESE GREENS WITH SCRAMBLED EGGS ····18
STIR-FRIED SPICY PORK ···································19
SPICY *TOFU* SZECHUAN STYLE ·····················20
BRAISED PRAWNS SZECHWAN STYLE ···········21
STIR-FRIED SNOW PEAS & MUSHROOMS ·······22
STIR-FRIED THAI BEEF ····································23
STIR-FRIED GEODUCK ······························24 · 25
STIR-FRIED CRABMEAT WITH *TOFU* ···············26
STIR-FRIED LETTUCE ·······································27
SHRIMP & VEGETABLES WITH EXOTIC SAUCE ····28
STIR-FRIED GROUND MEAT & EGGPLANT ·······29
VEGETABLES WITH FIVE-SPICE POWDER ········30
SAUTÉED LIVERS AND GARLIC STALKS ··········31
STIR-FRIED SHRIMP THAI STYLE ·····················32
ASSORTED-MUSHROOMS SAUTÉ ASIAN FLAVOR ····33
TOFU & VEGETABLES IN *MISO* SAUCE ···········34
CHICKEN WINGS WITH MUSHROOMS ···············35
STIR-FRIED CHINESE NOODLES WITH VEGETABLES ····36
CURRY FLAVORED POTATOES ··························37
SPICED BEEF & NUTS ·······································38
THAI NOODLES ··39
RED CURRY PASTE · VEGETABLE CURRY ····40 · 41
MASAMAN (MUSLIM) CURRY PASTE · BEEF CURRY ····40 · 41
ORANGE BEEF WITH BROCCOLI ·······················42
PORK POT STICKERS · DEEP-FRIED WON TON WITH SWEET & SOUR SAUCE ····43
GOLDEN OMELET ···44
BRAISED GINGER PORK ····································45
SAUTÉED LEMON FLAVORED SARDINES ·····46 · 47
STIR-FRIED THICK NOODLES · GRILLED *TERIYAKI* FISH ····48
GRILLED FISH FILLETS MALAYSIAN ·················49

STEAMING ···50

STEAMED LAYERED CABBAGE & GROUND CHICKEN ····51
CHICKEN SIU MAI ··52
SPICY STEAMED EGGPLANT ······························53
STEAMED WHOLE FISH CHINESE STYLE ··········54
STEAMED EGG CUSTARD ···································55
STEAMED CODFISH ···56
TWICE STEAMED SWEET RICE, *ZEN* STYLE ·······57

STEAMED CHICKEN & *TOFU* LOAF ···58
STEAMED FISH ···59
STEAMED MUSSELS WITH CILANTRO ·······························60
MEATBALLS WITH SWEET & SOUR SAUCE··························61
STEAMED TURNIPS, JAPANESE STYLE · VEGETARIAN DELIGHT SALAD ·············62
STEAMED CHICKEN BREAST CHINESE STYLE·····················63
MEATLOAF ···64
STEAMED PORK WITH VEGETABLES ·······························65

SIMMERING, BRAISING ···66
TWICE COOKED PRAWN DELIGHT ···································67
HOISIN SAUCE PORK ···68
CHINESE GREENS WITH CREAMY SAUCE ························69
BRAISED *SHIITAKE* MUSHROOMS & BABY CORN · BRAISED CHICKEN WINGS············70
STIR-FRIED PORK CANTONESE STYLE·······························71
CHICKEN *TERIYAKI* ··72
STIR-FRIED CHICKEN WITH OYSTER SAUCE ·····················73
SIMMERED SEA VEGETABLES ···74
STEAMED CLAMS WITH BASIL THAI STYLE ·····················75

DEEP-FRYING ··76
DEEP-FRIED FISH WITH SWEET & SOUR SAUCE···············77
WHOLE FISH WITH VEGETABLE SAUCE ····················78 · 79
DEEP-FRIED BEEF ROLLS ··80
TOFU TEMPURA ··81
DEEP-FRIED OYSTERS JAPANESE STYLE ·······················82
CRISPY DEEP-FRIED SOLE ··83
SPRING ROLLS · VEGETABLE ROLLS ····················84 · 85
PORK & ONION KABOBS ··86
CRISPY CHICKEN NUGGETS · SWEET & SOUR CHICKEN NUGGETS···············87
LOTUS ROOT *TEMPURA* DELIGHT ···································88
SEAFOOD *TEMPURA* ···89

BOILING, BLANCHING ···90
SPICY & SOUR MUSHROOM SOUP ·································91
SHRIMP BALL SOUP ··92
COCONUT MILK WITH *TOFU* ··93
CHINESE BROCCOLI WITH OYSTER SAUCE ·····················94
SHRIMP SALAD ···95

INGREDIENTS ···96~99
IMFORMATION
PREPARATION···100
PREPARATION & UTENSILS···101
BASIC CUTTING METHODS·······································102 · 103
INDEX ···104

BASIC COOKING INFORMATION

Today many areas of the world use the metric system and more will follow in the future. The following conversion tables are intented as a guide to help you.

General points of information that may prove valuable or of interest:

1 cup is equivalent to 240ml in our recipes: (American cup measurement)

1 American cup＝240ml＝8 American fl oz

1 British cup＝200ml＝7 British fl oz

1 Japanese cup＝200ml

1 tablespoon＝15ml   1 teaspoon＝5ml

TABLES CONVERTING FROM U.S. CUSTOMARY SYSTEM TO METRICS

Liquid Measures

U.S. Customary system	oz	g	ml
1/16 cup＝1T	1/2 oz	14g	15ml
1/4 cup＝4T	2 oz	60g	59ml
1/2 cup＝8T	4 oz	115g	118ml
1 cup＝16T	8 oz	225g	236ml
1 3/4 cups	14 oz	400g	414ml
2 cups＝1 pint	16 oz	450g	473ml
3 cups	24 oz	685g	710ml
4 cups	32 oz	900g	946ml

Liquid Measures

Japanese system	oz	ml
1/8 cup	7/8 oz	25ml
1/4 cup	1 3/4 oz	50ml
1/2 cup	3 1/2 oz	100ml
1 cup	7 oz	200ml
1 1/2 cups	10 1/2 oz	300ml
2 cups	14 oz	400ml
3 cups	21 oz	600ml
4 cups	28 oz	800ml

Weights   grams×0.035＝ounces   ounces×28.35＝grams

ounces to grams*	grams to ounces
1/4 oz＝ 7g	1g＝0.035 oz
1/2 oz＝ 14g	5g＝ 1/6 oz
1 oz＝ 30g	10g＝ 1/3 oz
2 oz＝ 60g	28g＝ 1 oz
4 oz＝115g	100g＝ 3 1/2 oz
6 oz＝170g	200g＝ 7 oz
8 oz＝225g	500g＝ 18 oz
16 oz＝450g	1000g＝ 35 oz

＊Equivalent

Linear Measures   inches×2.54＝centimeters   centimeters×0.39＝inches   in＝inch(es)   cm＝centimeter(s)

inches to centimeters	centimeters to inches*
1/2 in ＝ 1.27 cm	1 cm＝ 3/8 in
1 in ＝ 2.54 cm	2 cm＝ 3/4 in
2 in ＝ 5.08 cm	3 cm＝1 1/8 in
4 in ＝10.16 cm	4 cm＝1 1/2 in
5 in ＝12.7 cm	5 cm＝ 2 in
10 in ＝25.4 cm	10 cm＝ 4 in
15 in ＝38.1 cm	15 cm＝5 3/4 in
20 in ＝50.8 cm	20 cm＝ 8 in

The water boiling temperature given is at sea level.

Conversion factors:

$$C = (F - 32) \times \frac{5}{9}$$

$$F = \frac{C \times 9}{5} + 32$$

C＝Celsius   F＝Fahrenheit

Temperature

Fahrenheit (F) to Celsius (C)		Celsius (C) to Fahrenheit (F)	
freezer storage	−10°F＝−23.3°C	freezer storage	−20°C＝ −4°F
	0°F＝−17.7°C		−10°C＝ 14°F
water freezes	32°F＝ 0 °C	water freezes	0°C＝ 32°F
	68°F＝ 20 °C		10°C＝ 50°F
	100°F＝ 37.7°C		50°C＝122°F
water boils	212°F＝ 100 °C	water boils	100°C＝212°F
	300°F＝ 148.8°C		150°C＝302°F
	400°F＝ 204.4°C		200°C＝392°F

Deep-Frying Oil Temperatures

300°F−330°F(150°C−165°C)＝low	
340°F−350°F(170°C−175°C)＝moderate	
350°F−360°F(175°C−180°C)＝high	

Oven Temperatures

250°F−350°F(120°C−175°C)＝low or cool	
350°F−400°F(175°C−204°C)＝moderate or medium	
400°F−450°F(204°C−230°C)＝hot	
450°F−500°F(230°C−260°C)＝very hot	

GETTING TO KNOW YOUR WOK

The wok is the all-purpose cooking pot.

The traditional form of Chinese wok is a round or flat-bottomed pot made of heavy gauge carbon steel. The most common Oriental cooking methods include stir-frying, deep-frying, simmering, boiling, and steaming. Depending upon the method utilized, ingredients generally retain their natural flavor and nutrition with new and different tastes emerging from the use of each method.

Stir-Frying	*Steaming*	*Simmering*	*Deep-Frying*	*Boiling*

WOK WITH ONE HANDLE

The wok is deep, like a soup pot, so you can boil rice and make soup in it. The wok's rounded sides provide enough red-hot surface for stir-frying foods quickly, usually in 3 to 5 minutes. The wok with one handle is easy to move over high heat with one hand while you add new ingredients and stir with the other hand. Stir-frying cooks protein foods thoroughly while at the same time leaving them tender and juicy and vegetables retain the intense color and crisp texture.

The modern wok is made of light-weight stainless steel or aluminum with one or two handles. Also electric woks of various sizes and types are availables. They have the advantage of maintaining whatever temperatures you select, especially for steaming and deep-frying foods. For making a sauce, the electric wok with a nonstick surface is convenient.

The most functional size is the 14-inch(35cm) round wok.

The wok comes in various sizes, but the most functional for our purpose is the 14 inch(35cm) round wok. It is usually accompanied by a ventilated ring which serve to support the base

of the wok above a gas or an electric range-burner. Also it's fitted with a lid and an inner rack so you can steam vegetables and fish in it.

WOK WITH TWO HANDLES

This round or flat-bottomed wok has two handles, but usually one of them is long. This makes it easy to move the wok quickly over high heat with one hand while you add new ingredients. This type of the wok is especially helpful for steaming and deep-frying.

The great value of the wok is that it cooks foods quickly, retain natural juices, fresh tastes, and crispness.

Flat-bottomed wok & Round-bottomed wok

A flat-bottomed wok does not require a ring stand. It sits directly atop the electric and element and requires some adjustments during cooking as there is direct contact with the burner, resulting in much hotter temperatures. When using a gas range, the ring should be situated with the sides slanting downwards and the smaller opening supporting the wok. The round-bottom design of the wok directs the heat source to the center of the wok which gets very hot quickly.

The heat is then conducted rapidly and evenly throughout the rest of the wok. When using an electric range, the ring should placed securely over the burner, with the sides slanting upwards to allow the center of the wok closer proximity to the burner.

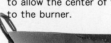

UTENSILS

Curved Spatula

This long handle utensil comes with a wide, curved edge which fits the curved bottom of the wok. Ingredients can be more readily tossed and removed using a curved rather than a straight-edged spatula.

This utensil comes with a long handle with a wide, curved edge which fits the curved bottom of the wok. Ingredients can be more readily tossed and removed using a curved rather than straight-edged spatula.

Ladle

This utensil with a long handle with round-bottomed shape fits the curved bottom of the wok. Ingredients can be readily pressed or tossed and soup can be removed using round shaped ladle.

Cleaver

The basic Chinese knife is the cleaver. It is used for cutting recipe ingredients and the same motion, transporting them to an awaiting wok or serving tray. The cleaver usually measures 3 inch to 4 inch (8cm to 10cm) wide and 8 inch (20cm) long. The thickness varies from thin cleavers for vegetable slicing to thick bone-chopping cleavers. A sharp cleaver is necessary to make the various cuts as discussed in the cooking methods discussed in the cooking methods section. Keep your cleaver sharp by using a sharpening stone and steel as often as needed. For other knives, see page 101.

Bamboo brush

This is made of bamboo sticks. It is used for cleaning the wok. Any bristle scrub brush used for non-stick pans will do the same job.

Bamboo Steamer

Bamboo steamers with two tiers and a cover are used for steaming foods. Select bamboo steamers which are round and smaller than the wok by 1½ inches. Metal steamers are also available, but unless a lot of food is steamed, a wok and steaming rack is sufficient. Steaming rack which is round, preferably made of metal, resembles a cake rack and is used to elevate plates of food above the boiling water in a wok while steaming. The vegetable steamer can be used for steaming food successfully. The steamer is adjustable according to the amount of food and size of wok you use.

Draining Rack

This is used in deep-frying or blanching vegetables to drain the oil or water from the food. This is made of heavy gauge carbon steel or stainless steel.

CHOPPING BOARD

The sharpness of the blade is affected by the chopping board you use. Wood gives the best surface. In Japan, cypress (hinoki) seen at *sushi* restaurants is one of the most common material. Willow or pine is also used. Plastic types are also available. After using, wash it quickly with sudsy water and wipe dry. To get rid of fishy odors on the chopping board, rub with sliced lemom, lemon juice, vinegar or salt before washing and then rinse well. Do not store it while still damp.

A COVER

The wok with a cover serve as a good steamer. Bamboo steamers with a cover have several tiers in which many dishes can be steamed simultaneously. The tiers and cover are set on top of wok containing boiling water. The size of the dome-shaped cover depends largely upon the diameter of the wok. Sometimes a 10-12 inch (25-30cm) cover to a wok may suffice. The convenience of a cover is readily apparent when it is necessary to steam ingredients using the wok.

SEASONING YOUR WOK

A newly purchased wok should be given special seasoning.

1.To remove the protective oil applied when manufactured, heat the wok until it begins to form a light haze.

2.Then fill it with water until almost full and bring to a boil. Discard the boiling water. Fill it with sudsy water and scrub. Rinse. Repeat 2-3 times.

3.Dry thoroughly. Then pour the oil down against the side of the wok and heat the oil over medium heat for several minutes.

4.Add some vegetable scraps and saute, rotating the wok to coat oil around sloping sides until vegetable scraps are almost burned black. Discard the vegetable scraps and oil. Wash the wok with hot water and clean and dry thoroughly.

WOK CARE & CLEANING

1.During the course of cooking a meal, the wok need only be cleaned with hot water, using a bristle scrub brush used for non-stick pans. Never scour your wok with harsh cleansers. When you are through using the wok, wash in sudsy water and rinse.

2.Dry over medium heat and rub a dab of oil on the inside surface to prevent rust. Eventually, with constant use, your wok will assume a darker color on the inside which results in smooth nonstick cooking. If rust appears, simply scrub clean and reseason. Any time the wok is used for steaming, it must be reseasoned afterward in order to prevent foods from sticking. However, only one coating of oil is necessary for reseasoning your wok.

TO MAKE YOUR WOK COOKING FAST AND EASY:

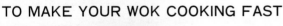

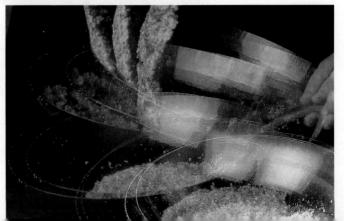

Too many ingredients in the wok can not be achieved for proper stir-frying, for instance, resulting in foods turning out soggy instead of crispy. The more ingredients in your wok, the more slowly they cook. So, in most stir-frying, we add ingredients one at a time, and push each cooked ingredients up onto the side of the wok before we add the next.

STIR-FRYING, SAUTÉING

This method of cooking combines the elements of high heat and quick, constant tossing to seal in the flavor and juices of meats and vegetables. Stir-frying cooks protein foods thoroughly at the same time leaving them tender and juicy. Vegetables stir-fried until barely tender retain their natural color and crisp texture.

Prepare all necessary ingredients before stir-frying. Slices are uniform in size so that they can be cooked even, and some vegetables require parboiling. Make sure that all vegetables are pat dry. Prepare all necessary seasonings before stir-frying.

STIR-FRYING, SAUTÉING

Heat the wok and swirl in oil.

Heat the wok until it barely gets hot and add oil (usually 2 tablespoons).
Rotate wok to coat oil around sloping sides.

Stir gently until aroma is fully extracted.

Add minced ginger root, garlic or green onion. Stir gently until the aroma is fully extracted, 20 to 30 seconds.
Timing and temperature will vary according to the type of wok selected and whether a gas or electric range is used.

Pour the liquid down against the side of the wok.

Stir-fry over medium high heat with vigorous arm action.

Actual stir-frying involves vigourous arm action in the constant stirring and tossing of the food. Actual cooking time will seldom exceed several minutes. Remember to adjust the temperature control for proper stir-frying temperature.

Some ingredients, such as carrot, broccoli and califlower may need parboiling before stir-frying.

Blanch the vegetables one at a time in a generous amount of rapidly boiling water.
As each vegetables is blanched, transfer it to an ice water bath to chill, then drain and follow the recipe.

Cut the vegetables uniform in sizes.

SHRIMP WITH VEGETABLES

INGREDIENTS: 4 servings

½ pound (225g) shrimp
½ cup pea pods, strings removed
2 tablespoons vegetable oil
1 teaspoon minced garlic
1 teaspoon minced fresh ginger root
¼ cup sliced green pepper
1 cup shredded cabbage
¼ cup sliced mushrooms
⅔ cup beansprouts
2 tablespoons minced green onion
2 tablespoons oyster sauce
1 tablespoon soy sauce
2 tablespoons *mirin*, Japanese sweet cooking wine
⅛ teaspoon salt
1 tablespoon sesame oil
Dash of pepper

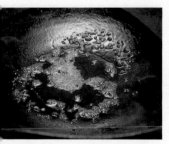

. Heat the wok to high heat; swirl in
tablespoons oil; add garlic and
resh ginger root; stir-fry for 30
econds.

2. Add shelled and deveined shrimp as shown below and stir-fry for 2 minutes. Remove and set aside.

3. Heat the wok to medium high heat; add all vegetables; stir-fry for 1 minute. Add remaining seasoning ingredients and combine.

4. Return cooked shrimp to the wok and combine.

SHRIMP PREPARATION

1. Cut off heads from shrimp. Remove shell from head end to tail.

2. Remove vein from the top of the shrimp.

3. Make a few incisions along the belly.

EGG FU YUNG

INGREDIENTS: 4 servings
6 eggs
4 green onions, chopped
½ pound (225g) bean-
sprouts, about 2 cups
2 dried *shiitake* mushrooms,
softened
1 ¼ cups cocktail shrimp,
shelled
1 tablespoon *sake*
1 teaspoon minced fresh ginger root
1 teaspoon salt
½ teaspoon pepper
4 tablespoons vegetable oil
Egg Fu Yung Sauce:
½ teaspoon salt
1 cup water
1 tablespoon cornstarch
1 tablespoon ketchup
2 teaspoons soy sauce
¼ teaspoon sugar

1. Prepare dried *shiitake* mushrooms as shown below. Heat the wok to medium high heat; swirl in 1 tablespoon of oil and add fresh ginger root. Stir-fry for 20 seconds. Add green onion, beansprouts and *shiitake* mushrooms. Stir-fry for 1 minute or until vegetables are crispy and tender.

5. Combine all egg fu yung sauce ingredients; bring sauce to a full boil, stirring constantly. Serve sauce over the egg fu yung.

2. Sprinkle *sake* over cocktail shrimp; add to the vegetables and season with salt and pepper. Transfer to a plate and let it cool.

DRIED SHIITAKE MUSH ROOMS PREPARETION

1. Soak *shiitake* mushrooms in water until soft which takes about 30 minutes.

3. Clean the wok; heat the wok to medium high heat; swirl in 1 tablespoon oil.

Beat eggs lightly. Ladle ½ portion of beaten eggs to the wok.

2. Trim off stems from mushrooms.

4. Add ½ potion of the vegetables and shrimp. Fry about 2 minutes, turn over and fry 3 more minutes to form a patty. Cut in half. Repeat the same process for another patty.

3. To soften dried *shiitake* mushrooms, add a pinch of sugar in luke-warm water for faster result.
Do not use hot water to prevent from shrinkage of the ingredients.

SWEET & SOUR PORK

INGREDIENTS: 4 servings

1 pound (450g) boneless pork loin, cut into 1½-inch (4cm) pieces

Marinade Sauce:
- 1 tablespoon soy sauce
- 1 teaspoon sesame oil
- 1 teaspoon *sake*
- 1 tablespoon *mirin*, Japanese sweet wine
- 1 teaspoon ginger juice, grated fresh ginger root
- Dash of pepper
- 1 tablespoon hot bean paste or 1 teaspoon 7-spice powder

1 small can pineapple chunks, drained and the juice reserved

Cornstarch for dusting

1 green pepper, cut into chunks

Oil for deep-frying

Sweet & Sour Sauce:
- ⅓ cup rice vinegar
- pineapple juice from the can plus water to make 1 cup juice
- 2 tablespoons soy sauce
- 3½ tablespoons sugar
- 1 tablespoon cornstarch

1. Marinate pork pieces in marinade sauce for 30 minutes.

2. Coat pork with cornstarch.

3. Heat deep-fry oil to 360°F (180°C) ; deep-fry pork for approximately 5 minutes or until done. Drain on paper towels.

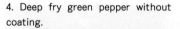

4. Deep fry green pepper without coating.

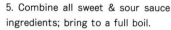

5. Combine all sweet & sour sauce ingredients; bring to a full boil.

6. Mix in deep-fried pork, green pepper and pineapple chunks and quickly toss together.

※Fresh pineapple can be used instead of canned pineapple.

15

SEAFOOD FRIED RICE

1. In the wok, mix water and *sake*; bring to a boil. Add seafood mix and cook for 1 minute. Drain and set aside.
Trim off stems from mushrooms and slice thin.

2. Heat the wok to medium heat; swirl in 1 tablespoon oil.
Pour beaten eggs and make scrambled eggs. Sprinkle some salt and pepper to taste and set aside.

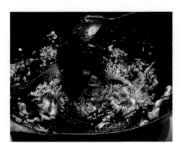

3. Swirl in 2 tablespoons oil in the wok; add *shiitake* mushrooms and green onion; stir-fry over medium heat for 1 minute.

4. Add cooked rice and mix and stir well. Stir-fry for a few minutes until rice is heated through.
Pour soy sauce in and add seafood mix and eggs. Continue to cook for 2 to 3 minutes over medium heat.

SEAFOOD FRIED RICE

INGREDIENTS: 2 to 3 servings
2 cups cooled cooked unseasoned rice
4 ounces (115g) frozen seafood mix or frozen seafood of your choice
2 tablespoons *sake* or white wine
⅓ cup water
2 fresh *shiitake* mushrooms
2 green onions, chopped
2 eggs, beaten
1 tablespoon vegetable oil
Salt & pepper to taste
2 tablespoons vegetable oil
½ teaspoon light-color soy sauce

FRIED RICE

INGREDIENTS: 4 servings
4 cups cooled cooked rice
3 eggs, beaten
2 tablespoons shortening or 2 tablespoons vegetable oil
2 dried *shiitake* mushrooms, softened (see page 14)
4 green onions, chopped
4 tablespoons frozen peas or mix vegetables
1 teaspoon salt
¼ teaspoon pepper
½ cup diced barbecued pork or cooked ham
1 tablespoon light-color soy sauce
4 to 6 tablespoons vegetable oil
¼ teaspoon curry powder (optional)

TIPS FOR FRIED RICE

1. Heat the wok to medium high heat and rotate wok to coat oil.

2. Adjust temperature while stir-frying. Press fried rice to the sides of the wok with a ladle.
Repeat same process several times.

FRIED RICE

1. Heat the wok to medium high heat; swirl in 2 tablespoons shortening; pour beaten eggs and make scrambled eggs. Set aside.

2. Soften *shiitake* mushrooms; trim off hard stem ends and slice *shiitake* mushrooms.

3. Heat the wok to medium high heat; swirl in 2 tablespoons oil and add green onion, *shiitake* mushrooms and mix vegetables; stir-fry for 1 minute.

4. Sprinkle salt and pepper over vegetables; add diced meat. Swirl in another 2 to 3 tablespoons oil; add cooked rice.
Stir-fry for 4 to 5 minutes.

5. Add soy sauce and mix well, using more oil as needed.

6. Add scrambled eggs and curry powder and stir well, adjusting temperature as needed.

1. Heat the wok to medium high and add oil.
2. Roll the oil around to cover the cooking surface of the wok.

3. Pour lightly beaten eggs at once. Stir eggs in the constant motion.

INGREDIENTS: 4 servings

1 tablespoon vegetable oil
4 eggs
2 tablespoons vegetable oil
½ cup minced green onion
1 tablespoon minced fresh ginger root
1 ¼ pounds Chinese greens (bok choy), cut into 2-inch (5cm) pieces
1 cup soup stock
2 tablespoons soy sauce
1 tablespoon *sake* or cooking wine
1 teaspoon sugar
½ teaspoon salt
1 tablespoon cornstarch dissolved in 2 tablespoons water

1. Heat the wok to medium high (375°F); swirl in 1 tablespoon oil; pour lightly beaten eggs and make scrambled eggs as shown above and set aside.

2. Swirl in 2 tablespoons oil; add green onion and ginger root. Stir-fry 1 minute.

3. Add Chinese greens; stir-fry 1 minute; add soup stock, soy sauce, *sake*, sugar and salt. Bring to a boil.
Add scrambled eggs.

4. Pour the cornstarch mixture; stir until the sauce thickens and clears.

18

STIR-FRIED SPICY PORK

INGREDIENTS: 4 servings
½ pound (225g) pork
Marinade Sauce:
  1 teaspoon *sake* or white cooking wine
  1 tablespoon soy sauce
  2 teaspoons cornstarch
2 green peppers, cut into slivers
¼ cup minced green onion
1 teaspoon grated fresh ginger root
1 clove garlic, minced
2 tablespoons vegetable oil
1 ½ teaspoons hot bean paste
1 tablespoon soy sauce
1 teaspoon *sake* or white cooking wine
½ teaspoon sugar
½ teaspoon salt
½ teaspoon sesame oil
1 ½ tablespoons hoisin sauce (optional)

1. Slice pork thin against the grain. Then cut into slivers.
Coat pork with marinade sauce for 5 minutes.

2. Heat the wok to medium high heat; swirl in 1 tablespoon oil. Add pork and stir-fry until done.
Remove from the wok and set aside.

3. Add 1 tablespoon vegetable oil to the wok, stir-fry ginger root, garlic and hot bean paste for 30 seconds over medium high heat.

4. Add shredded green pepper and stir to combine ingredients.
Add soy sauce, *sake* sugar, salt, sesame oil and hoisin sauce.
Return pork to the wok.
5. Mix in green onion and stir-fry for 30 seconds to 1 minute to thoroughly combine the ingredients. 19

SPICY TOFU SZECHUAN STYLE

INGREDIENTS: 4 servings

14 ounces (400g) firm *tofu* (see below for preparation)
4 dried *shiitake* mushrooms, softened
7 ounces to 8 ounces (200g to 250g) ground pork or beef

Ⓐ
- 1 tablespoon soy sauce
- ½ teaspoon sugar
- 1 teaspoon *sake* or cooking wine

2 green onion, chopped
1 clove garlic, minced
2 teaspoons minced fresh ginger root
2 dried chili pepper, seeded and chopped (or 2 teaspoons hot bean paste)

Ⓑ
- 1 tablespoon red *miso* paste
- ½ teaspoon soy sauce
- Pinch of sugar
- 1 tablespoon ketchup
- ¾ cup soup stock (or shiitake soaking water)

½ tablespoon sesame oil
1 to 2 tablespoons vegetable oil
2 teaspoons cornstarch dissolved in 1 tablespoon water for thickening

---

1. Trim hard stem ends from *shiitake* mushrooms; thinly slice it.
Cut *tofu* into ¾-inch (2cm) cubes. Set aside.

2. Mix ground meat with Ⓐ ingredients.

3. Heat the wok to high heat; swirl in 1 tablespoon vegetable oil. Add garlic, ginger root and chili pepper; stir-fry for 30 seconds.

4. Add seasoned ground meat, chopped green onion, *shiitake* mashrooms; stir-fry for 2 minutes or until meat is well cooked.
Add sesame oil.

5. Mix Ⓑ ingredients; pour into meat mixture.
Adjust heat to medium; bring to a boil. Add *tofu* and mix carefully not to break *tofu*.

TOFU PREPARATION

6. Thicken with cornstarch mixture over medium heat to desired thickness.
Turn off heat.

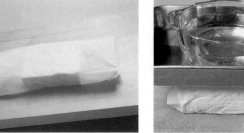

1. Wrap *tofu* in gauze or paper towels.

2. Place between two boards and let stand to drain. For faster result place *tofu* on several layers of towels on cutting board and top with water-filled bowl. Change towels often.

BRAISED PRAWNS SZECHWAN STYLE

INGREDIENTS: 4 servings

1 pound (450g) prawns
2 tablespoons vegetable oil
1 clove garlic, minced
½ small onion, chopped
1 teaspoon minced fresh ginger root
1 to 2 tablespoons hot bean paste
4 tablespoons ketchup
3 tablespoons *sake* or white cooking wine
1 tablespoon sugar
Pinch of salt
2 green onions, minced, green part only (option)

1. Prepare prawns as shown below. Rinse and pat dry.
(The shell of the prawn retain the moisture when cooked.)

2. Heat the wok to medium high heat; add garlic, onion and ginger root; stir-fry for 20 seconds.

3. Add prawns; stir-fry for 1 minute. Add hot bean paste, ketchup, *sake*, sugar and a pinch of salt.
Bring to a boil, cooking prawns for 1 minute.
Toss in green onions.

PRAWNS PREPATION

1. Cut off heads from prawns.

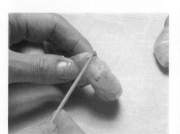

2. Remove vein from the top of the prawns.

3. Cut off tips of tail ends and gently press out water to prevent oil splattering while prawns are stir-fried.

Ingredients: 2 to 3 servings

4 ounces (115g) snow peas
1 pack *shimeji* mushrooms
2 medium dried *shiitake* mushrooms, softened
2-inch (5cm) long leek, chopped
½ dried chili pepper, chopped
1½-inch (7mm) piece fresh

ginger root, minced
1 tablespoon vegetable oil

(A) ⎰ 1 tablespoon soy sauce
⎟ 1 teaspoon oyster sauce
⎟ 1 tablespoon *sake* or *mirin*
⎟ Japanese sweet cooking wine
⎰ Dash of white pepper
⅛ teaspoon sesame oil

1. Prepare snow peas as shown below.
Slice off hard ends of *shimeji* mushrooms; parboil for 30 seconds. Set aside.

2. Soften *shiitake* mushrooms; trim off hard stem ends and slice thin.

3. Heat the wok to medium high heat; swirl in the vegetable oil and add ginger root and chili pepper. Stir-fry for 30 seconds.

4. Add chopped leek, then snow peas, *shimeji* and *shiitake* mushrooms. Stir-fry until snow peas turn bright green in color.

5. Mix Ⓐ ingredients; pour in the wok and stir-fry 1 to 2 minutes.

6. Swirl in sesame oil; stir once and remove from heat.

TO TRIM OFF SNOW PEA

1. Trim off hard ends and remove strings from the snow peas.

INGREDIENTS: 4 servings

2 tablespoons vegetable oil
2 cloves garlic, minced
1 teaspoon crushed red pepper
½ pound (225g) flank steak, thinly sliced
½ onion, sliced
1 cup broccoli flowerets, cooked

1 zucchini, cut into thin rounds
6 to 8 basil leaves
1 tablespoon oyster sauce
2 tablespoons fish sauce
1 teaspoon sugar
Some ground pepper and salt to taste
1 tablespoon chopped cilantro (option)

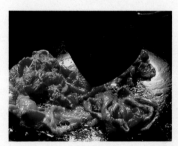

1. Heat the wok to medium high heat; swirl in 2 tablespoons oil. Add garlic and crushed red pepper; stir-fry for 20 seconds. Add beef and stir-fry for 3 minutes.

2. Add sliced onion, cooked broccoli, zucchini and stir-fry until onion is tender.

3. Add basil leaves, oyster sauce, fish sauce, sugar, salt and pepper, stir to combine. Add chopped cilantro. Serve hot.

INGREDIENTS: 4 to 6 servings

1 medium size geoduck clam (horse clam)
1 tablespoon *sake* or white cooking wine
1 teaspoon soy sauce
1 teaspoon cornstarch
1 clove garlic, minced
1 tablespoon minced fresh ginger root
1 green pepper
½ cup sliced *shiitake* mushrooms
3 ounces (90g) pea pods, strung, rinsed and patted dry
½ cup sliced onion
1 tablespoon vegetable oil
¼ teaspoon grated lemon peel
2 to 3 tablespoons vegetable oil
½ teaspoon sesame oil
1 teaspoon hot bean paste
¼ teaspoon fish sauce
2 mint leaves
Salt & pepper to taste

1. Prepare geoduck as shown below.

4. Remove strings from pea pods.

5. Heat the wok to medium high heat; swirl in 1 tablespoon oil. Add garlic and ginger root; stir-fry 30 seconds.
Add vegetables and *shiitake* and stir-fry for about 1 minute until vegetables are crisp tender. Remove and set aside and keep warm.
6. Clean the wok, heat to medium high heat; swirl in 2 tablespoons oil.

2. Cut open lengthwise. Make a few incisions lengthwise. Cut diagonally into thin, ⅛-inch (½ cm) slices.

3. Combine clam slices with *sake*, soy sauce and cornstarch.

7. Add clam slices and grated lemon peel. stir-fry for 30 seconds.

8. Add sesame oil, hot bean paste and fish sauce. Stir and mix.

9. Add vegetables *shiitake* stir to combine ingredients. Toss in mint leaves and salt and pepper to taste and serve hot. Do not overcook clam slices or they will become tough.

GEODOCK PREPARATION

1. Insert a sharp knife between the shell halves and pry open. Insert a sharp knife between flesh and shell, pry out the flesh.

2. Discard stomach and pull off neck.

3. Wash thoroughly to remove sand and skin. Remove the transparent membrane.

4. Cut off the black hard end.

25

INGREDIENTS: 2 to 3 servings

1 can crabmeat, drained and with the cartilage removed
12 ounces (345g) firm *tofu*, drained
¼ teaspoon grated fresh ginger root
½ cup pea pods or 3 ounces (90g) broccoli flowerets, cooked
1 tablespoon vegetable oil
1 tablespoon *sake* or white wine
¼ teaspoon salt
½ teaspoon sugar
¼ cup soup stock
1 tablespoon light-color soy sauce
2 teaspoons cornstarch dissolved in 1 tablespoon water
1 teaspoon minced green onion

1. Cut *tofu* into halves lengthwise, then cut into halves crosswise. Slice into ½-inch (1.2cm) thick pieces.

2. Heat the wok to medium high heat, swirl in 1 tablespoon vegetable oil, add grated ginger root; stir-fry for 20 seconds. Add crabmeat and *sake*; stir-fry for 1 minute.

3. Add *tofu*, soup stock, salt, sugar, and soy sauce. Adjust heat to medium and stir-fry for 2 to 3 minutes.

4. Add cooked broccoli and pour cornstarch mixture in the wok. Stir until thickened and cleared. Sprinkle minced green onion on top.

BROCCOLI PREPARATION

1. Cut off hard stem ends from broccoli.

2. Make incisions as shown.

3. Blanch the broccoli in a generous amount of rapidly boiling salted water for 1 minute.

4. Transfer it to ice water bath to chill, then drain.

STIR-FRIED LETTUCE

INGREDIENTS: 3 to 4 servings
1 head iceburg lettuce
½ tablespoon vegetable oil
¼ teaspoon sesame oil

4 water chestnuts, chopped
1 tablespoon minced parsley

1 teaspoon *mirin*, Japanese sweet cooking wine
½ teaspoon sugar
½ teaspoon light-color soy sauce
Salt and pepper to taste
1 chicken bouillon cube, dissolved in ½ cup water
1 teaspoon cornstarch, dissolved in 1 tablespoon water

1. Trim off the bottom of the lettuce. Cut into quarters.

2. Heat the wok to medium high heat; swirl in vegetable and sesame oil. Add lettuce and stir-fry for 30 seconds.

3. Add water chestnuts and stir-fry for another 30 seconds.
Season with *mirin*, sugar, soy sauce, salt and pepper.
Pour the soup stock down the side of the wok and bring to a boil.

4. Mix in parsley. Add the cornstarch mixture; stir until thickened and cleared.

INGREDIENTS: 4 servings

½ pound (225g) large shrimp
4 ounces (115g) Chinese char
or bok choy
⅓ carrot, thinly sliced
1 small onion, thinly sliced
1 green pepper, thinly slice
lengthwise
½ cup sliced mushrooms
2 mint leaves; chopped
¼ cup cilantro, chopped

A {
  1 tablespoon lemon gras
  chopped
  1 tablespoon curry powder
  ¼ teaspoon chili pepper
  1 tablespoon water
  6 tablespoons lime juice
  3½ tablespoons fish sauce
  1 tablespoon sugar
  2 tablespoons vegetable c
  olive oil
}

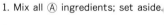

1. Mix all Ⓐ ingredients; set aside.

2. Cut off heads from shrimp
devein and shell, leaving tail
attached.

3. Cut chard into 1-inch (2.5cm) in length.

4. Heat the wok to medium high heat; swirl in oil. Add shrimp; stir-fry for 1 minute. Remove shrimp from the wok. Set aside.

5. Heat the wok to medium high heat, again; add vegetables except mint and cilantro leaves. Stir-fry until all vegetables are crisp tender. Pour the Ⓐ ingredients; toss and stir-fry for 1 minute over high heat.

6. Add shrimp and mint & cilantro leaves. Toss and serve hot.

INGREDIENTS: 4 servings

½ pound (**225g**) eggplant, or **4** small Japanese eggplants
2 tablespoons vegetable oil

I tablespoon minced garlic
I tablespoon minced fresh ginger root
I dried chili, seeded and chopped

½ pound (**225g**) ground beef or pork

Ⓐ {
I tablespoon hoisin sauce or black salted hot beans
2 tablespoons soy sauce
I tablespoon rice vinegar
¼ teaspoon sugar
I cup soup stock
}

2 teaspoons sesame oil

1. Cut ends off from eggplants. Dice them into ¾-inch (2cm) cubes. Soak in water to avoid discoloration.

2. Heat the wok to medium high heat; swirl in 2 tablespoons oil. Add garlic, ginger root, ground meat and cook until pork is well done.

3. Add chopped chili; stir-fry for 30 seconds.

4. Combine all Ⓐ ingredients; pour into the wok. Drain eggplant and add to the meat. Reduce temperature to medium and cook until sauce is reduced in half and eggplants are tender.

5. Add sesame oil for flavor.

VEGETABLES WITH FIVE-SPICE POWDER

INGREDIENTS: 4 servings

12 ounces (340g) cauliflower, trimmed and cut into walnuts size nuggets

1 cup beansprouts

6 ounces (180g) carrots, cut into 1/8-inch (2.25mm) thick rounds

1 stalk celery, sliced diagonally

4 green onions, cut diagonally

2 tablespoons vegetable oil

1 tablespoon minced fresh ginger root

2 tablespoons fish sauce

1/4 teaspoon five-spice powder

Pinch of salt and dash of pepper

1 teaspoon sesame oil

1. Blanch the vegetables one at a time in rapidly boiling unsalted water; immerse them in ice water, then drain. Set aside.

2. Heat the wok to high; swirl in 2 tablespoons vegetable oil. Add fresh ginger root; stir-fry for 20 to 30 seconds. Add the vegetables; stir-fry for 2 minutes. Adjust the heat to medium high so vegetables will not scorch.

3. Stir in fish sauce, five-spice powder, salt and pepper. Drizzle 1 teaspoon sesame oil down the side of the wok; toss lightly for 10 to 20 seconds. Serve immediately.

SAUTÉED LIVERS AND GARLIC STALKS

INGREDIENTS: 4 servings

1 pound (450g) chicken or calf liver, sliced into ¼-inch (7mm) thick
½ teaspoon ginger juice,
1 tablespoon *sake* or white cooking wine
2 tablespoons cornstarch
⅓ pound (150g) garlic stalks
2 tablespoons chopped preserved Szechuan vegetable
3 tablespoons vegetable oil
¼ teaspoon sesame oil
⅓ cup soup stock
1 tablespoon soy sauce
1 teaspoon *mirin*, Japanese sweet cooking wine
1 teaspoon sugar
½ teaspoon rice vinegar or lemon juice

LIVER PREPARATION

1. Trim any membrane from edges of liver slices; soak in water and rinse under running water until water clears.

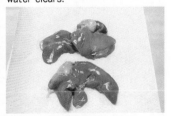

2. Drain and pat dry with paper towels.

1. Prepare liver as shown above.

2. Combine liver with ginger juice and *sake* for 2~3 minutes. Coat liver with cornstarch.

3. Cut garlic stalks into 2½-inch (6.5cm) in length.
Heat the wok to medium heat; swirl in 1 tablespoon vegetable oil; add garlic stalks and stir-fry for a few minutes until crisp tender. Remove from the wok and set aside.

4. Pour another 2 tablespoons of vegetable oil in the wok; add the liver and cook over meduim heat for 4 minutes, turning once, until crisp and brown on the outside. Add sesame oil, soup stock, soy sauce, *mirin*, sugar and rice vinegar; mix well.

5. Add preserved Szechuan vegetable and garlic stalks and toss and stir-fry for 1 minute.

※Kimchee can be used instead of garlic stalks.

INGREDIENTS: 2 servings

½ pound (225g) shrimp, shelled, deveined
¼ medium onion, sliced
¼ cup sliced mushrooms
2 tablespoons vegetable oil
1 tablespoon minced garlic
1 teaspoon curry powder
1 tablespoon fish sauce
1 tablespoon oyster sauce
1 tablespoon sugar

1. Heat the wok; swirl in oil and add garlic; sauté for 30 seconds over high heat.

2. Add shrimp and stir-fry 1 minute; and sliced onion and mushrooms and stir-fry until the onion is soft.

3. Add all seasoning ingredients; toss and stir for 2 minutes.
Serve hot with steamed rice if you prefer.

INGREDIENTS: 2 servings
3 ounces (90g) each button mushrooms, *shimeji* and *enoki* mushrooms
4 *shiitake* mushrooms
1 clove garlic, minced
2 tablespoons olive oil
¼ teaspoon salt
Dash of pepper
1 tablespoon minced parsley
1 teaspoon grated lemon or *yuzu* citron peel
¼ teaspoon light-color soy sauce
⅛ teaspoon hot bean paste

1. Trim off hard stem ends from mushrooms. Slice button mushrooms and *shiitake* mushroooms. Separate each strand of *shimeji* and *enoki* mushrooms.

2. Heat the wok to medium high heat; swirl in olive oil. Add minced garlic and stir gently until the aroma is fully extracted, for 20 to 30 seconds. Add all mushrooms and stir-fry for 1 to 2 minutes.

3. Season with salt and pepper. Adjust heat to medium; add grated lemon or *yuzu* citron peel. Turn off the heat.

4. Add light-colored soy sauce and hot bean paste. Sprinkle minced parsley. Combine and serve immediately.

INGREDIENTS: 4 to 6 servings

2 blocks firm *tofu*, well drained

1 can (net weight 15¼ ounces, 425g) straw mushrooms, drained

9 ounces (90g) cooked bamboo shoots, thinly sliced

1 green pepper, thinly sliced

1 cup chopped green onion

3 dried chili pepper, seeded and chopped

1 clove garlic, minced

1 teaspoon minced fresh ginger root

2 to 3 tablespoons vegetable oil

Miso Sauce:

1 tablespoon red *miso*

2½ tablespoons low-salt soy sauce

1 teaspoon sugar

1 tablespoon *sake* or white cooking wine

1. Cut *tofu* into 1-inch (2.5cm) cubes. Set aside.

2. Heat the wok to high heat; swirl in 1 tablespoons oil.
Add *tofu* and stir-fry for 2 minutes or until lightly browned on all sides. Set aside.

3. Swirl in 2 tablespoon oil; add garlic, ginger root and chili pepper; stir-fry for 30 seconds over high heat. Add green onion, straw mushrooms, bamboo shoots, green pepper; stir-fry for 2 minutes over medium heat.

4. Add *tofu* and all *miso* sauce ingredients; toss and stir-fry for 1 minute, adjusting heat to medium high. Turn off heat.

INGREDIENTS: 4 servings

1 pound (450g) chicken wings

Marinade Sauce:
- 1 tablespoon soy sauce
- ½ tablespoon sesame oil
- 1 tablespoon *sake*, Shaoshing or other cooking wine
- 1 tablespoon cornstarch

2 tablespoons vegetable oil

2 green onion, sliced diagonally
4 fresh *shiitake* mushrooms, sliced or 1 cup canned sliced mushrooms drained
1 can, 15 ounces (425g) straw mushrooms, drained
1 teaspoon grated ginger root
½ teaspoon garlic, minced
2 teaspoons soy sauce
½ cup soup stock
A pinch of salt
1 teaspoon *sake*, Shaoshing or other cooking wine
1 teaspoon cornstarch dissolved in
1 tablespoon water

TIPS: CORNSTARCH FOR THICKENING

When adding cornstarch mixture to thicken a sauce or other seasoning, push all ingredients to the side and pour the liquid down against the side of the wok, as you poured in the oil.

A good stir-frying temperature is 375°F (190°C). If the temperature is too high, the food will burn which case a lower temperature adjustment is in order, On the other hand, if the temperature is too low, ingredients do not fry, but will soak in the oil and will lose their flavor.

1. Combine chicken wings with marinade sauce and let stand for 30 minutes.

2. Heat the wok over medium high heat; swirl in 2 tablespoons oil. Stir-fry chicken wings until done or all sides are browned. Set aside.

3. Add oil if necessary to the wok; stir-fry ginger root and garlic for 20 seconds over medium high heat. Add *shiitake* and straw mushrooms, mushrooms, green onion, soup stock, sake or wine, salt and soy sauce; stir-fry for 1 minute.

4. Return the chicken wings and soy sauce to the wok; stir to combine. Bring to a boil. Thicken with cornstarch mixture.

INGREDIENTS: 2 servings

¼ pound (115g) chinese noodles
¼ pound (115g) shrimp, shelled

Ⓐ
- ½ teaspoon grated fresh ginger root
- 1 clove garlic, minced
- 1½ teaspoons soy sauce
- 2 teaspoons cornstarch

1 tablespoon vegetable oil
¼ cups sliced onion
2 cups shredded cabbage
2 fresh *shiitake* mushrooms, thinly sliced
1 green pepper, thinly sliced
1 cup beansprouts
8 pea pods

Ⓑ
- 2 tablespoons soy sauce
- 1 teaspoon *sake* or mirin
- 1 teaspoon rice vinegar
- 1 tablespoon sesame oil
- 1 tablespoon white miso paste

TIPS FOR STIR-FRY SHRIMP

1. Heat the wok to high; swirl in vegetable oil.

2. Add shrimp and stir-fry quickly. The cornstarch makes shrimp crispy outside and retain the moisture inside when cooked.

1. Cook noodles in a generous amount of rapidly boiling water just until tender. Rinse and drain noodles; set aside. Combine shrimp with Ⓐ ingredients.

2. Heat wok; swirl in 1 tablespoon oil and stir-fry shrimp for 1 minute over high heat as shown above right.

3. Add all vegetables and stir-fry for 2 to 3 minutes.

4. Reduce heat, and add noodles. Toss and mix well. Combine all Ⓑ ingredients.

Pour Ⓑ ingredients in the wok and stir-fry until well mixed.

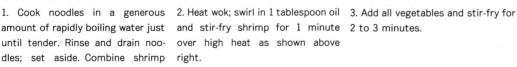

CURRY FLAVORED POTATOES

INGREDIENTS: 2 servings
1 ½ pounds (460g) potatoes
1 onion
2 to 3 tablespoons vegetable oil
½ teaspoon curry powder
1 teaspoon soy sauce
1 teaspoon hot bean paste
⅓ cup soup stock

1. Scrub potatoes in cold water. Peel with a vegetable peeler. Cut potatoes into ⅛-inch (3mm thick rounds). Soak in water and drain. Slice onion thin.

2. Heat the wok to medium heat; swirl in 2 tablespoons oil. Add sliced onion; stir-fry until onion is tender soft.

3. Add potatoes and stir-fry until potatoes are lightly browned.

4. Add curry powder, soy sauce, hot bean paste and soup stock. Stir once and cook until vegetables are tender.

INGREDIENTS: 4 servings

½ pound (225g) flank steak

Marinade Sauce:

⌈ 1 tablespoon soy sauce
  2 teaspoons *mirin*, Japanese sweet cooking wine
  2 teaspoons *sake*
⌊ 2 teaspoons vegetable oil

1 tablespoon cornstarch
3½ ounces (100g) peanuts or cashew nuts, roasted
1½ green peppers
3½ ounces (100g) cooked bamboo shoots
2 *shiitake* mushrooms, softened, or 4 button mushrooms
1 dried red chili pepper, seeds removed and chopped
2 tablespoons vegetable oil
1 clove garlic, minced
1 tablespoon minced fresh ginger root

⌈ 1 tablespoon white *miso*, soy bean paste
  1 teaspoon sugar
  1 teaspoon soy sauce
Ⓐ ½ teaspoon hot bean paste
  Dash of pepper
  ½ cup *shiitake* soaking water
  2 teaspoons cornstarch
⌊ ½ teaspoon sesame oil

1. Slice beef into ½-inch (1.5cm) by 2-inch (5cm) slices. Combine with marinade sauce and set aside for 10 to 20 minutes. Coat with 1 tablespoon cornstarch.

2. Toast peanuts or cashew nuts in the wok without oil and set aside.

3. Cut green peppers and bamboo shoots into chunks.
Trim hard stem ends of shiitake mushrooms and slice.

4. Heat the wok to medium high heat; swirl in 1 tablespoon oil.
Add garlic, ginger root and red chili pepper and stir-fry for 20 seconds.
Add marinated beef; stir-fry for 2 to 3 minutes.
Remove from the wok and set aside.

5. Add remaining 1 tablespoon oil to the wok; add green peppers; bamboo shoots and *shiitake* mushrooms. Stir-fry for 5 minutes over medium high heat.
Return beef to the wok and combine.

6. Combine all Ⓐ ingredients; stir in beef and cook for 2 to 3 minutes.
Add toasted peanuts. Serve hot.

THAI NOODLES

INGREDIENTS: 4 servings

8 ounces (225g) bean threads or rice noodles
3 tablespoons vegetable oil
1 tablespoon minced garlic
¼ pound (115g) thinly sliced meat (beef or pork)
2 tablespoons fish sauce
2 tablespoons soy sauce
1 teaspoon sugar
1 tablespoon paprika

1 green onion, cut into 1 inch (2.5cm) length
1 cup broccoli flowerets, steamed
⅔ cup beansprouts
¼ cup ground roasted peanuts

Garnishes, optional:
Cilantro sprigs, lime or lemon wedges

1. Prepare bean threads as shown below.

2. Heat the wok to over medium high heat, swirl in the oil; add minced garlic. Stir-fry for 1 minute; add meat and stir-fry until done.

BEAN THREADS PREPARATION

3. Add fish sauce, soy sauce, sugar, paprika and bean threads.

4. Stir-fry and thoroughly combine with seasonings for a few minutes over medium high heat.
Add green onion, broccoli and beansprouts. Stir-fry, adding a small amount of water if required.
Mix in peanuts after vegetables are cooked. Combine thoroughly. Garnish and serve hot.

1. Soak bean threads in lukewarm water for 1 hour or until soft.
Cut bean threads with kitchen scissors.

2. Bring to a boil; drain and set aside.

RED CURRY PASTE

This marvelous paste can be stored in a jar for future use. It goes well with beef, pork, chicken and fish as well as vegetables.

Makes about 1 cup

10 whole dried long red chili peppers, seeded and coarsely chopped
¼ cup chopped onion
¼ cup minced garlic
2 tablespoons chopped fresh lemon grass (or 3 tablespoons lemon grass powder)
1 tablespoon chopped fresh galanga (ginger root)
1 tablespoon minced fresh kaffir lime peel
½ teaspoon ground mace or cumin powder
½ teaspoon cardamon seeds
½ teaspoon pepper corns, freshly ground
2 tablespoon chopped fresh coriander (cilantro) root
1 teaspoon caraway seeds
1 teaspoons shrimp paste
1 teaspoon salt
3 tablespoons vegetable oil

1. Combine all ingredients except oil in a blender and process until smooth.

2. Heat the wok to medium high heat; add 3 tablespoons oil. Slowly stir-fry curry paste ingredients for 5 minutes until it is fragrant. Remove and store in a jar for future use.

VEGETABLE CURRY

INGREDIENTS: 4 servings

3 cups cooked rice (see page 101)
1 whole pineapple (or 1 cup canned crushed pineapple)
14 ounces (400g) coconut milk
Ⓐ
2 tablespoons red curry paste
¼ cup fish sauce
1½ tablespoons sugar
1 tablespoon maggie sauce
1 tablespoon lemon juice
1 pound (450g) assorted steamed vegetables (zucchini, carrot, califlower, broccoli, potatoes).
Dash of white pepper
2 tablespoons toasted cashews or peanuts
4 tablespoons raisins
Garnish: Thinly sliced-green pepper strips (optional)

1. Cut a whole pineapple in half lengthwise.
Remove all pineapple flesh but ½-inch (1.5cm) layer from inside of pineapple halves. Crush pineapple flesh and save the pineapple boat to use as a serving dish.
2. Steam vegetables of your choice.

3. Combine all Ⓐ ingredients and bring to a boil.
Add vegetables and crushed pineapple; cook for a few minutes.

4. Add peanuts and raisins. Turn off heat and mix thoroughly.

5. Combine cooked rice with ⅓ portion of vegetable curry.

6. Stuff rice into pineapple boats and garnish with green pepper strips. Serve with curry sauce.

MASAMAN (MUSLIM) CURRY PASTE

This paste is the base for Masaman beef curry.

Makes about ½ cup

4 to 5 whole dried long red chili peppers, seeded
½ cup chopped onion
½ cup coarsely chopped garlic
1 tablespoon chopped lemon grass
2 slices fresh galanga (or 4 slices dried)
2 shallots, chopped
5 pepper corns, freshly ground
2 tablespoons coriander seeds (or 1 tablespoon coriander powder)
1 teaspoon ground cumin
1 teaspoon nutmeg
1 teaspoon ground mace
1 teaspoon cinnamon powder
1 teaspoon ground cloves
1 tablespoon star anise powder (or 10 cardamom seeds)
4 bay leaves
5 tablespoons vegetable oil

BEEF CURRY

INGREDIENTS: 4 servings

3 cups cooked rice (see page 101)
14 ounces (400g) canned coconut milk
1 tablespoon masaman curry paste
¼ cup fish sauce
2 tablespoons sugar
¼ teaspoon white pepper
1 pound (450g) beef, cut into serving pieces
¼ cup minced garlic
¼ cup chopped onion
5 to 8 Kaffir lime leaves
4 cups cooked rice (see page 101)
Garnishes:
5 to 8 fresh basil leaves
2 tablespoons roasted peanuts, chopped

1. Heat the wok to medium heat; add 5 tablespoons oil and cook chili peppers, onions and garlic until golden brown.

2. Combine fried ingredients and all remaining ingredients in a blender and process until smooth. Store in a jar for future use.

BEEF CURRY

1. Combine ½ can of coconut milk with curry paste, fish sauce, sugar and white pepper; thoroughly combine. Add beef, chopped garlic and onion. Bring to a gentle boil over medium heat and cook until beef is done.

2. Add remaining coconut milk and lime leaves; heat through.
Garnish with basil leaves and chopped peanuts just before serving.
※Substitute dried fresh mint leaves for kaffir lime leaves if unable to find fresh kaffir lime leaves.

ORANGE BEEF WITH BROCCOLI

INGREDIENTS: 2 servings

½ pound (225g) flank steak, sliced into ½-inch (1.27cm) thick slices

1 tablespoon soy sauce

½ teaspoon grated fresh ginger root

1 tablespoon cornstarch

1 cup broccoli flowerets, steamed

1 orange peel, thinly sliced

1 orange, sliced into thin rounds

1 tablespoon soy sauce

1 teaspoon *mirin*, Japanese sweet rice wine

1 teaspoon sugar

2 teaspoons cornstarch dissolved in 1 tablespoon water

1. Blanch broccoli (see page 26).

2. Cut orange peel into thin slices. Cut 1 orange into thin rounds. Set aside.

3. Marinate beef slices in the mixture of soy sauce and grated ginger root for 3 to 4 minutes; coat with cornstarch.

4. Heat the wok to medium high heat; swirl in 1 tablespoon oil.
Add beef and stir-fry for 1 minute. Add broccoli and orange peel; stir-fry for 2 to 3 minutes.

5. Add soy sauce, *mirin* and sugar stir once.
Add cornstarch mixture and sti until thickened and cleared.

6. Place orange slices on a servin plate and place stir-fried beef an broccoli on top.

PORK POT STICKERS

INGREDIENTS: Makes 30 to 40 pot stickers
30 to 40 large won ton wrappers
Filling:
- 1 pound (450g) ground pork
- 2 cups finely chopped *nappa* cabbage
- ¼ cup chopped onion
- 1 tablespoon grated fresh ginger root
- 1 teaspoon light-color soy sauce
- 2 teaspoons sesame oil
- ½ teaspoon sugar
- 1 teaspoon *sake* or cooking wine
- 2 tablespoons cornstarch

2 to 3 tablespoons vegetable oil
2 cups water

WRAPPING FOR PORK POT STICKERS
Place 2 tablespoons filling in center of wrapper, wet edge and seal to form a half circle. press edges with fork as shown.

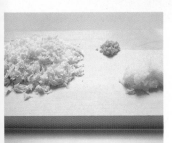

1. Prepare all filling ingredients.

2. Mix the filling in a bowl.

3. Place filling in center of wrapper and to shape as shown above.

4. Heat the wok with small amount of oil to medium high heat and fry pot stickers until brown on all sides. Pour some water, cover and cook until liquid is absorbed.
Repeat with the rest of pot stickers. Serve with soy sauce, vineger or soy sauce and hot chili oil mixture.

DEEP FRIED WON TON WITH SWEET & SOUR SAUCE

INGREDIENTS: Makes 1½ cups
30 Prepared pork pot stickers
Sweet & Sour Sauce
- 2 tablespoons cornstarch
- ⅔ cup sugar
- ⅓ cup rice vinegar
- 1 teaspoon *sake* or cooking wine
- ⅔ cup water
- 1 teaspoon soy sauce
- 3 tablespoons ketchup

Oil for deep-frying

1. Heat deep-frying oil in the wok to 325°F (165°C).
Deep fry pot stickers until golden brown.
Drain oil.

2. Mix all sweet & sour sauce ingredients. Stir constantly while cooking over medium heat. Cook until thickened.

GOLDEN OMELET

TIPS

1. Heat the wok to medium; swirl in oil to coat the sides of the wok.

2. Pour the egg mixture and tilt the wok to distribute eggs to prevent sticking from bottom of the wok.

INGREDIENTS: 2 servings

6 eggs
¼ pound (115g) ham
1 small tomato
½ small onion
½ green pepper

Ⓐ ⎰ ½ teaspoon tabasco sauce
1 tablespoon soy sauce
1 teaspoon sugar
⅛ teaspoon pepper
⎱ ⅛ teaspoon salt

1½ tablespoons vegetable oil

1. Lightly beat eggs. Mix Ⓐ ingredients with eggs.
Chop ham, tomato, onion and green pepper into small pieces.

2. Heat the wok to medium; coat with thin film of oil.
Stir-fry half portion of ham and vegetable mixture until onion is cooked.

3. Pour half amount of egg mixture to cover the bottom of cooked vegetables as shown above. When eggs are almost set, lift one end and fold into half. Turn over and cook 30 seconds over medium low heat.
Repeat another half portion.

INGREDIENTS: 2 servings

12 ounces (200g) boneless pork loin, thinly sliced

Marinade sauce:

- 2 ½ tablespoons soy sauce
- 1 tablespoon *mirin*, Japanese cooking wine
- ½ tablespoon grated fresh ginger root
- Dash of pepper

2 tablespoons vegetable oil

Garnish:

Small green pepper, thinly sliced lengthwise or 4 Japanese green chili

TO PREVENT SHRINKAGE

1. Remove excess fat from pork slices. Make slits as shown right. Combine all marinade sauce ingredients; marinate pork slices for 20 minutes.

2. Heat the wok to medium heat; swirl in oil; add pork slices. Sauté until brown on both sides, adding more oil if necessary.

3. Add sliced green pepper or prick green chili two to three places to prevent shrinking; stir-fry for 1 minute. Pour in remaining marinade sauce in the wok and bring to a full boil and remove from heat.

1. Make slits along fat to prevent shrinkage while cooking.

INGREDIENTS: 4 servings

4 fresh sardines
8 *shiso* leaves, beefsteak plant, perilla, or spinach leaves
1 teaspoon white cooking wine
1 tablespoon fresh ginger juice from grated fresh ginger root
1 tablespoon low-salt soy sauce
2 tablespoons all-purpose flour for coating
1 teaspoon grated lemon peel
2 tablespoons olive oil

1. Prepare sardines as shown below. Sprinkle wine on fish fillets and set aside.

2. Mix ginger juice with soy sauce. Marinate fish fillets for 10 minutes.

3. Mix flour with grated lemon peel. Place one fillet skin side down on a cutting board. Put 2 *shiso* leaves on top. Place another fillet skin side up on top. Dust with flour mixture.

4. Heat oil in the wok over medium heat; add sardine fillets and sauté on both sides until done. Cut into serving pieces.

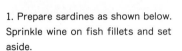

SARDINES PREPARATION

1. Remove scales from tail end. Insert knife under pectoral fin at right angles and cut off head.

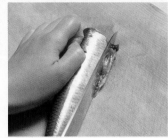

2. Make a slit in belly to anal fin.

3. Remove entrails.

4. Wash under running water. Wipe dry.

5. Insert knife through back.

6. Separate meat along backbone.

7. To make two fillets, one with bone, insert knife through the back and work along backbone.

8. Cut small bones along center line.

9. Remove skin.

STIR-FRIED THICK NOODLES

1. Heat 1 tablespoon oil in wok over medium heat. Stir-fry noodles until partially browned. Set aside and keep warm.

3. Add onion, green onion and cabbage; stir-fry for 5 minutes or until all vegetables are tender.

2. Heat 1 tablespoon vegetable oil in wok over medium heat; stir-fry pork until color turns to pale.

4. Mix curry powder with water; add curry powder mixture and stir well. Add soy sauce and noodles; stir well. Serve hot.

INGREDIENTS: 1 serving

1 tablespoon vegetable oil
1 package fresh thick noodles (*Udon*)
1 slice loin pork or 2½ ounces (75g) pork, cut into serving pieces
½ onion, cut into chunks
1 green onion, cut into 1½-inch (4cm) in length
1 cabbage leaf, chopped
⅓ cup beansprouts
1 tablespoon curry powder dissolved in 1 tablespoon water
1 tablespoon soy sauce
1 tablespoon vegetable oil

GRILLED TERIYAKI FISH

INGREDIENTS: 4 servings

4 yellow tail, cod or salmon fillets

Marinade Sauce:
4 tablespoons soy sauce
1 teaspoon sugar
2 tablespoons *mirin*, Japanese sweet cooking wine
1 teaspoon *sake* or white wine
½ tablespoon grated fresh ginger root
1 tablespoon vegetable oil

2. Heat vegetable oil in a wok to medium heat; cook fish fillets, turning once, until done.

1. Marinate fish fillets in marinade sauce for 10 minutes, turning once.

3. Remove the fish fillets to individual plates. Cook remaining sauce in the wok and pour over fillets.

INGREDIENTS: 4 servings
4 fish fillets, swordfish, tuna, cod or red snapper

Marinade Sauce:
- 1 egg, lightly beaten
- 1 teaspoon ground turmeric
- ¼ teaspoon chili pepper
- 1 small onion, chopped
- 1 clove garlic, minced
- ½ teaspoon minced parsley
- 1 tablespoon lemon juice

1 to 2 tablespoons all-purpose flour
2 tablespoons vegetable oil
1 lemon, cut into wedges

1. Marinate fish fillets in marinade sauce for 1 hour.

2. Dust fillets with all-purpose flour.

3. Heat the wok to medium heat; swirl in vegetable oil.

Add fish fillets and cook on both sides until done.

Serve hot with lemon wedges.

STEAMING

Steaming is one of the most nutritious, not to mention convenient methods of cooking foods, retaining more nutrients and natural flavor than other conventional means of cooking.

There are many different types of steamers available. A wok with a cover serve as a good steamer. Multi-tiered bamboo steamers may be purchased. All steamers operate according to the same basic principle. The efficient circulation of steam is of paramount importance.

STEAMING

Fill the wok with water.

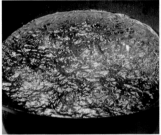

Pour water in the wok or pot so that the water level stands 1 inch (2. 5cm) below the steaming rack or dish of food. Bring the water to a full boil.

Place the steaming rack after water fully boiled.

Place the dish of food atop of the steaming rack. Cover and bring to a full boil (or full steam).

Coat thin film of oil to prevent from sticking.

Use heatproof dishes only for steaming. Coating thin film of oil may prevent food from sticking to the dish.

Check the water level, Add hot water as shown.

Check the water level when longer steaming times are necessary. To lift a lid, lift the lid away from you so that steam will not cover your face directly. Bamboo steamers have several tiers in which many dishes can be steamed simultaneously. For example, the bottom pot functions to cook soup stock while the two tiers are used to steam two other separate dishes. In this manner, many dishes may be steamed at one time saving both time and energy.

INGREDIENTS: 4 servings

4 large *nappa* cabbage (Chinese celery cabbage)
2 fresh *shiitake* mushrooms
1 pound (450g) ground chicken

Ⓐ
- ½ teaspoon grated fresh ginger root
- ½ teaspoon salt
- 2 teaspoons light color soy sauce
- ½ teaspoon *sake* or cooking wine
- 1 teaspoon *mirin*, Japanese sweet cooking wine

Garnish (optional):
lime, *yuzu* citron or lemon peel
2 large eggs
1 tablespoon all purpose flour
A few drops of vegetable oil

Sauce:

Ⓑ
- 1 ⅓ cups soup stock
- ¼ teaspoon salt
- 1 tablespoon light color soy sauce
- ⅛ teaspoon sugar

2 teaspoons cornstarch dissolved in 1 tablespoon water

1. Parboil cabbage in water 2 to 3 minutes; place on a bamboo mat or basket to drain off water.
Trim off stem ends of *shiitake* mushrooms; cut into small pieces.

2. Mix Ⓐ ingredients with ground chicken.

3. Lightly beat eggs; mix with ground chicken and mushrooms. Add 1 tablespoon flour and mix well; divide into three equal parts.

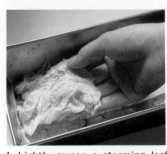

4. Lightly grease a steaming loaf pan; place cabbage leaf in greased pan.

8. Mix Ⓑ ingredients; bring to a boil. Add cornstarch mixture and stir until it thickens and clears.
Pour over hot cooked cabbage.

5. Pour one portion of meat mixture and place another cabbage leaf on top. Repeat the same process.

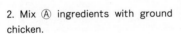

6. Steam for 15 to 20 minutes over high heat. Add water if necessary during steaming.

7. Turn up-side-down and unmold. Slice into serving sizes.

INGREDIENTS: Makes 25 siu mai

25 *siu mai* wrappers

Filling:

⟨ ½ pound (225g) ground chicken
¼ cup chopped bamboo shoots
¼ cup chopped softened *shiitake* mushrooms
2 tablespoons chopped water chestnuts
1 tablespoon *sake* or cooking wine
2 tablespoons cornstarch
1 egg white, lightly beaten
1 tablespoon soy sauce
1 tablespoon sesame oil
½ teaspoon sugar
½ teaspoon salt
⅛ teaspoon pepper ⟩

25 green peas

1. Soften *shiitake* mushrooms. (See page 14)

2. Combine all filling ingredients.

3. Wrap filling with wrapper as shown below.

4. Place on steaming plate and steam for 10 to 20 minutes over high heat.

SIU MAI PREPARATION

1. Hold wrapper by finger circle.

2. Squeeze into a round.

3. Place 1 heaping tablespoon filling in center of wrapper.

4. Gather edges of wrapper around filling. Flatten the bottom, squeeze the center and smooth off the top with wet fingers. Place 1 green pea on top.

52

SPICY STEAMED EGGPLANT

INGREDIENTS: 4 servings
4 Japanese eggplants or 2 small egg plants
4 ounces (115g) ground chicken
1 tablespoon minced fresh gingerroot
1 small onion, chopped
1 teaspoon fennel seeds
1 teaspoon ground coriander
2 teaspoons ground cumin
½ teaspoon turmeric
1 cup tomato sauce
1 teaspoon hot bean paste
½ tablespoons vegetable oil
1 teaspoon sesame oil
Garnish:
cilantro sprigs

1. Cut stems off from tip of eggplant. Cut eggplant into fourths lengthwise. Each cut should start at just below the stem and extend to the bottom.

2. Set eggplants on a steaming plate.
Place in a steamer, cover, bring to a full boil, reduce heat to medium high and steam for 7 minutes. Place on a serving plate.

3. Heat oil in the wok, add ginger root, onion and ground chicken: stir-fry over medium high (375°F) heat for a few minutes.

4. Add rest of all ingredients except cilantro. Cook 2 to 3 minutes. Turn off heat.
Pour over eggplants. Garnish with cilantro sprigs.

53

INGREDIENTS: 4 servings
1 whole fish 2 to 2¼ pounds
(900g to 1kg)
4 slices fresh ginger root
1 leek or ½ bunch green
onion, chopped
1 tablespoon soy sauce
1 tablespoon *sake* or white
cooking wine
Dash of pepper
Sauce:
 4 tablespoons chopped
 green onion
 2 tablespoons fresh ginger
 root, fine shred
 1 teaspoon *sake* or white
 cooking wine
 1 tablespoon soy sauce
3 tablespoons vegetable oil
⅛ teaspoon sesame oil
Granish:
Cilantro, chopped

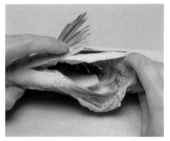

1. Prepare fish as shown below.
Wash under running water.
Stuff 1 tablespoon fresh ginger root
and 2 tablespoons chopped onion in
belly.

2. Place fish on a steaming plate;
cut 3 slashes to the bone on both
sides. Sprinkle *sake*, soy sauce and
pepper on top.

3. Place remaining chopped green
onion and ginger root on top. Place
in a steamer and steam for 25
minutes. Add hot water into the
wok if necessary during steaming.

4. Remove green onion and ginger
root from top and inside belly; also
drain excess liquid from the plate.

5. Spread sauce ingredients evenly
on top of steamed fish. Heat vegetable and sesame oil to medium
high. Pour over the fish. Garnish
with cilantro leaves.
The ingredients should sizzle.

FISH PREPARATION

1. Remove hard scales from tail end.

2. Make a short slit in belly.

3. Remove entrails. Scrape out any
entrails left and dark blood with
knife.

STEAMED EGG CUSTARD

INGREDIENTS: 4 servings

3 large eggs

Ⓐ
- 1 ⅔ cups soup stock
- ¼ teaspoon salt
- 1 teaspoon *mirin* Japanese sweet cooking wine
- 1 teaspoon light-color soy sauce

Fillings:

2 fresh *shiitake* mushrooms

4 water chestnuts (canned)

8 small cocktail shrimp, shelled

1 teaspoon *sake*

A pinch of salt

Some *mitsuba* leaves or some spinach leaves

1. In a small sauce pan, add Ⓐ ingredients; cook over medium heat until salt dissolves. Set aside to cool. Trim stem ends of mushrooms and cut in half. Cut water chestnuts into fourths.

2. Sprinkle *sake* and salt on shrimp. Blanch cocktail shrimp in boiling water for 20 seconds. Drain.

3. Beat eggs and mix with soup stock; strain with cloth to make creamy custard.

4. Place *shiitake* mushrooms and water chestnut fillings in bottom of steaming cups. Pour egg mixture in cups.

5. Place in a bamboo steamer and cover; steam for 2 to 3 minutes over medium low heat. Add shrimp and *mitsuba* leaves; adjust heat to medium high and steam for 7 to 8 minutes or until set. Test for doneness as shown right.

THE TESTING FOR DONENESS EGG CUSTARD

1. A bamboo skewer comes out clean after testing for doneness.

※For regular steamer, place egg custard in a hot steamer, lay kitchen towel between the steamer and lid.

STEAMED CODFISH

INGREDIENTS: 2 servings
2 small slices cod fish fillets or white meat fish
1 bunch *enoki* mushrooms
2 fresh *shiitake* or button mushrooms, thinly sliced
2 mild green chilies
2 teaspoons light-color soy sauce
½ teaspoon *mirin*, Japanese sweet cooking wine
¼ teaspoon *sake* or cooking wine
⅛ teaspoon salt
¼ teaspoon fresh ginger juice from grated fresh ginger
2 sheets aluminum foil, 10-inch (25cm) X 6-inch (15cm)

1. Cut off hard stem ends of *enoki* mushrooms and cut in half.

2. Place fish fillet in center of foil. Arrange mushrooms around the fillet. Add green chili.

3. Season each fish with soy sauce, *mirin*, *sake*, salt and ginger juice.

4. Fold to seal and make a boat shape.
Place the foil wrapped fish in a steamer and steam over high heat for 10 minutes or until fish is flaky and green chili is tender.

INGREDIENTS: 2 servings

1 cup sweet rice (glutinous rice)
1 deep-fried *tofu* pouch
½ package *shimeji* mushrooms
1 package *enoki* mushrooms
1 fresh *shiitake* mushroom
2 ounces (60g) canned colt foot, fiddle heads or cooked edible plants, drained

Cooking Broth:

⎰ ½ cup dashi or vegetable soup stock
⎱ 1 teaspoon light-color soy sauce
⎰ ½ teaspoon sugar
⎱ A pinch of salt
⎰ ¼ teaspoon *mirin* or *sake*

1. Rinse sweet rice until water runs clear. Allow rice to soak in water for 1 hour; drain.
Place a clean cloth in a steaming rack; spread rice out to an even layer.

2. Place in a steamer and cover and steam for 15 to 20 minutes over high heat. Add water if necessary during steaming.

3. Dip fried *tofu* pouch in hot water to remove excess grease. Drain and pat dry with paper towel. Slice and chop into small pieces.

4. Trim stem ends of *shimeji*, *enoki* and *shiitake* mushrooms. Slice *shiitake* mushrooms.

5. Combine *tofu* pouch, mushrooms and vegetables with cooking broth; cook over medium high heat until most of broth is absorbed.

6. Turn off heat and thoroughly mix in rice.
Place in individual steaming bowls or on bamboo leaves.

Place in a steamer and steam for 15 minutes.
※Can be made a head in large portion and kept in the freezer.

STEAMED CHICKEN & TOFU LOAF

INGREDIENTS: 4 servings

Makes 6×5¼×1¾-inch (15×14×4.5cm) loaf

5 ounces (140g) ground chicken

Ⓐ
- 1 teaspoon *sake* or white cooking wine
- 1 tablespoons light-color soy sauce
- Dash of white pepper
- ⅛ teaspoon poultry seasoning
- 2 tablespoons minced green onion

2 blocks (16 ounces, 450g each) firm *tofu*, well drained

Ⓑ
- 1 egg white, lightly beaten
- 2 teaspoons salt
- 1½ tablespoons cornstarch

Some vegetable oil for coating loaf pan

1. Combine ground chicken with Ⓐ ingredients.

2. Drain *tofu* well. Crumble *tofu* with fingers or electric mixer. Add all Ⓑ ingredients and blend until tofu is smooth in texture.

3. Lightly grease the loaf pan or lay plastic wrap into loaf pan.
Place seasond ground chicken mixture.

4. Pour half of *tofu* mixture on top.

5. Place other half of chicken mixture and flatter out.
Pour other half of *tofu* mixture and flatter out.

6. Steam for 3 minutes over high heat then turn heat to medium, and continue steaming for 15 minutes. Add water if necessary during steaming. Slice into serving pieces.

STEAMED FISH

INGREDIENTS: 2 servings
2 slices fish fillets
1 tablespoon *sake* or white wine
⅛ teaspoon salt
2 fresh *shiitake* mushrooms
2 sheets (2-inch, 5cm square)
kombu, kelp
1 block *tofu*
Cooking Broth:
- 2 sheets (2-inch, 5cm squre)
  kombu kelp
  1 ½ cups water
  2 tablespoons light-color soy
  sauce
Garnish:
2 tablespoons grated fresh *dai-kon* radish
2 teaspoons lemon or lime juice
Lemon peel
(optional)

1. Sprinkle fish fillets with *sake* and salt and let stand for 10 minutes.

2. Trim hard stem ends of *shiitake* mushrooms; cut in halves. Wipe kelp with a damp cloth or paper towels. Cut tofu into bite size pieces.
Place kelp in the wok or in a small sauce pan and add 2½ cups water; heat over medium heat until boiling point, but remove the kelp just before the water actually boils. Add 2 tablespoons light-color soy sauce. Set aside.
Slice kelp into julienne strips as garnish if you desire, and set aside.

3. Place kelp piece in an individual steaming dish; place fish fillet, *tofu* and *shiitake* mushrooms on top. Pour the half portion of cooking broth in the dish.

4. Steam for 10 minutes over high heat. Garnish with grated *daikon* radish, lemon juice, lemon peel and kelp.

STEAMED MUSSELS WITH CILANTRO

INGREDIENTS: 2 servings
½ pound (225g) fresh mussels,
cleaned and beard removed
1 tablespoon olive oil
1 clove garlic, minced
1 green onion, chopped
1 tablespoon white wine
Dash of white pepper
Cilantro for garnish

1. Prepare mussels as shown below.

2. Heat the wok to medium high heat; swirl in oil.
Add garlic and stir-fry for 30 seconds and add mussels.

MUSSELS PREPARATION

3. Add green onion, wine and pepper. Cover and steam until mussel shells open up.

4. Garnish with cilantro and serve.

1. Scrub mussels with stiff brush.

2. Trim off beard from mussels.

※Clams are delicious alternative to mussels or use a combination of both.

INGREDIENTS: 4 servings

1 pound (450g) ground pork or lean ground beef
4 tablespoons chopped water chestnuts
1 tablespoon chopped green onion
1 tablespoon chopped onion
1 teaspoon ginger juice or grated fresh ginger root
1 tablespoon soy sauce
1 tablespoon *sake* or white cooking wine
¼ teaspoon salt
1 egg, lightly beaten
1 tablespoon cornstarch

Sweet & Sour Sauce:
  ¼ cup rice vinegar
  ¼ cup sugar
  ½ teaspoon chili pepper
  3 tablespoons ketchup
  1 tablespoon *sake* or white cooking wine
  ¼ teaspoon salt
  1 teaspoon sesame oil
  ½ cup water
  2 tablespoons cornstarch

1. Combine all but sweet & sour sauce ingredients thoroughly. Stir meat and mix well. Shape into 1-inch (2.5cm) meatballs. Wet fingers with water to keep mixture from sticking.

2. Place in steaming plates and steam for 20 to 25 minutes.

3. Combine all sweet & sour sauce ingredients thoroughly in the wok.

4. Stir and bring to a boil, adding steamed meatballs.

VEGETARIAN DELIGHT SALAD

INGREDIENTS: 4 servings as a side dish

5 bunches turnip leaves
½ tablespoon salt
1¼ cups finely shredded *daikon* radish (optional)

Dressing:

Ⓐ { 1 tablespoon juice from squeezed *yuzu* citron (½ *yuzu* citron)
¼ teaspoon light-color soy sauce
¼ teaspoon sesame oil

1. Blanch turnip leaves in a generous amount of rapidly boiling water for 30 seconds. Transfer it to an ice water bath to chill and retain bright color, then drain. Place in a plastic bag and add ½ tablespoon salt. Seal and leave for several hours in a refrigerator.

2. Rinse under running water; drain well. Chop into small pieces.

3. Mix Ⓐ dressing ingredients; toss with turnip leaves.

INGREDIENTS: 4 to 6 servings

1 pound 7 ounces to 1½ pounds (650g to 700g) turnips
7 ounces (200g) *surimi* or raw shrimp, shelled
1 teaspoon *sake* or cooking white wine
1 teaspoon light-color soy sauce
2 small fresh *shiitake* mushrooms
1 tablespoon frozen peas
2 small eggs
1 teaspoon salt
1 teaspoon sugar
2 teaspoons *mirin*, Japanese sweet cooking wine

Sauce:

Ⓐ { 1¼ cups soup stock (*dashi*, vegetable or chicken)
1 tablespoon light-color soy sauce
2 tablespoons mirin (sweet cooking wine)
1 teaspoon grated fresh ginger root
2 teaspoons cornstarch dissolved in 2 tablespoons water

Garnish:

Grated lemon peel or *yuzu* citron peel
wasabi paste

1. Peel turnips and grate them. Set aside.

2. Season *surimi* or shrimp with *sake* and soy sauce.
Chop *shiitake* mushrooms into small pieces.

3. Lightly beat eggs; add grated turnips, *surimi* or shrimp, *shiitake* mushrooms, peas, salt, sugar and *mirin*. Stir egg mixture with chopsticks or fork but do not beat.

4. Pour into 4 steaming cups. Place in a bamboo steamer and cover. Steam over moderate heat for 15 to 20 minutes or until set.

5. In a small saucepan, mix Ⓐ sauce ingredients; bring to a boil. Add cornstarch mixture; stir until thickened. Pour sauce over the steamed turnips. Garnish with lemon peel. Serve with grated *wasabi* paste if desired.

INGREDIENTS: 2 servings

1 chicken breast, deboned
1 tablespoon Chinese rice wine, Shaoshing wine
1 teaspoon salt
2 to 3 slices fresh ginger root
1 tablespoon minced green onion
2 anise stars

Sauce:
¼ teaspoon crushed garlic
1 tablespoon soy sauce
½ teaspoon sesame oil
¼ teaspoon hot chili oil
Some white pepper

1. Lay chicken breast flat and cut into halves.
Make 3 slashes to the skin.
Rub 1 teaspoon salt into chicken skin.

2. Place chicken breasts on a large steaming platter.
Sprinkle with rice wine and top with anise stars, ginger root slices and minced green onion.
Steam in a steamer over high heat for 20 to 25 minutes.

3. Combine all sauce ingredients, and serve chicken with the sauce.

MEATLOAF

INGREDIENTS: 4 servings
Makes 9×5×3-inch (23×13×8cm) loaf

10 ounces (300g) lean ground beef

Ⓐ
- 1½ teaspoons fresh grated ginger root
- 1 teaspoon salt
- ½ tablespoon *sake* or cooking wine
- 4 teaspoons cornstarch
- 2 teaspoons soy sauce
- 1 egg, lightly beaten

½ cup cooked mixed vegetables

Some vegetable oil

1. Prepare a steamer.

2. Combine Ⓐ ingredients with ground beef. Mix vegetables with meat.

3. Lightly grease a loaf pan; pour meat mixture in greased pan. Flatten the surface.

4. Steam for 15 minutes over high heat or until a bamboo skewer comes out clean after testing for doneness.

STEAMED PORK WITH VEGETABLES

INGREDIENTS: 4 servings
½ pound (225g) pork roast
¾-inch (2cm) square fresh ginger root, thinly sliced
2 anise stars
I leek, cut into 4-inch (10cm) in lengths
2 cups sliced green peppers
I cup cauliflower flowerets

Meat Sauce:
2 tablespoons soy sauce
I tablespoon *sake* or white cooking wine
½ teaspoon sugar
¼ teaspoon grated fresh ginger root
½ clove garlic, crushed
¼ teaspoon sesame oil
I teaspoon oyster sauce
I tablespoon cornstarch dissolved in 2 tablespoons water

1. Place pork roast, sliced ginger root, anise stars and leek in the wok and pour enough water to cover the pork roast. Heat the wok to a boil and reduce temperature and cover and simmer pork roast for 30 minutes.
Remove and allow to cool.

2. Slice pork; place on a steaming plate and steam for 5 minutes.

3. Arrange green peppers and cauliflower around the pork slices; steam for 7 to 10 minutes until vegetables are tender.

4. Combine meat sauce ingredients; bring to a boil. Pour over the pork.

SIMMERING, BRAISING

Simmering and braising foods require special preparation.
Some ingredients need parboiling to remove the harsh or bitter taste and rawness. Also, some ingredients take longer to cook. These ingredients are sometimes re-cooked in different pans, then added to the simmering liquid.

SIMMERING, BRAISING

Use light seasoning.

Simmered food can be served as a single dish or as one-pot dish. The ingredients and simmering liquid for the one-pot dishes are prepared ahead of time and arranged attractively on larger platters. Use light seasoning for simmering liquid. The less the better. You can always add more later. In general add sugar or *mirin* first, then salt, rice vinegar (if recipe calls for it) and soy sauce.

Adjust temperatures

Remember to control simmering temperature so that the liquid can be slowly absorbed into the ingredients.

Skim froth during simmering.

Generally add soy sauce last in cooking.

Add soy sauce last in cooking and stir well. If simmering for a longer time, use a deep pot that holds an ample amount of simmering liquid.

TWICE COOKED PRAWN DELIGHT

INGREDIENTS: 2 servings
8 large prawns
1 tablespoon *sake* or white wine
Simmering Broth:
  1 tablespoon light-color soy
  sauce
  1 tablespoon *mirin*, Japanese sweet cooking wine
  1 teaspoon sugar
  1 teaspoon rice vinegar
  1 teaspoon grated fresh ginger root
  1 teaspoon lemon juice
  1 tablespoon ketchup
½ teaspoon sesame oil

1. Remove vein from the top of the prawns carefully. Rinse and pat dry (do not shell the prawns). The shell of the prawn retains the moisture when cooked.

2. Place the prawns in a steaming plate; sprinkle with *sake*. Steam for 15 minutes over high heat.

3. Clean the wok; add all simmering broth ingredients and bring to a boil.

4. Return the steamed prawns to the wok. Simmer over medium heat until broth is absorbed. Swirl in sesame oil just before removing from the stove.

HOISIN SAUCE PORK

INGREDIENTS: 4 servings
½ pound (225g) boneless pork loin
½-inch square cube fresh ginger root, thinly sliced
1 green onion, cut into 2-inch in length
2 green peppers
1 leek, cut into, 4-inch (10cm) in lengths
1 tablespoon vegetable oil

1 teaspoon minced ginger root
1 tablespoon minced garlic

Cooking Sauce:

1 tablespoon hoisin sauce
1 tablespoon soy sauce
½ tablespoon hot bean paste
1 tablespoon *sake* or cooking wine
1 teaspoon sugar
Pepper to taste

1. In the wok, place pork loin, ginger and leek, and pour enough water to cover the pork roast. Bring to a boil and adjust temperature to low. Simmer for 30 minutes. Skim froth while simmering. Remove and allow to cool.

2. Slice pork into 1-inch (2.5cm) cubes.

3. Cut green peppers into 1-inch (2.5cm) cubes. Slice onion. Heat the wok to medium high heat; swirl in 1 tablespoon oil. Add ginger root and garlic and stir-fry for 30 seconds. Add green peppers and onion; stir-fry until vegetables are crisp tender. Remove and set aside.

4. Add pork cubes in the wok and stir-fry on high heat until light brown.
Combine all cooking sauce ingredients and add to the pork and stir-fry for 1 minute or until sauce is reduced.

5. Return green peppers and onion to the wok and combine.

INGREDIENTS: 2 servings

1 pound (450g)
Chinese greens (bok choy), cut into 2-inch (5cm) pieces
1 tablespoon minced fresh ginger root
1 teaspoon sesame oil
⅔ cup soup stock
⅓ cup milk
Dach of white pepper
¼ teaspoon salt
¼ teaspoon light-color soy sauce

1 teaspoon *sake* or cooking wine
1 teaspoon cornstarch dissolved in 1 teaspoon water

CHINESE GREENS PREPARATION

1. Trim off hard stem ends. Wash and pat dry. Cut into 2-inch (5cm) in length.

1. Prepare Chinese greens as shown above.

2. Heat the wok to medium high heat, swirl in the sesame oil; add ginger root and stir-fry 30 seconds. Pour in soup stock and bring to a boil.

3. Add Chinese greens and bring to a boil, again.

4. Add pepper, salt, soy sauce, *sake* and milk.

5. Add cornstarch mixture just before boiling point. Stir until the sauce thickens.

BRAISED SHIITAKE MUSHROOMS & BABY CORN

2. Heat the wok to medium high (375°F); swirl in the vegetable and sesame oil. Add *shiitake* mushrooms and stir-fry 1 minute.

3. Add Ⓐ ingredients and cook over medium heat until most broth is absorbed.

4. Add baby corns. Stir and mix well for 1 minute.

INGREDIENTS: 4 servings

8 large *shiitake* mushrooms
1 can, 8 ounces (230g) young corns, drained
1 tablespoon vegetable oil
⅛ teaspoon sesame oil
Simmering Broth:
  1 cube chicken bouillon

Ⓐ
⅔ cup *shiitake* soaking water or tap water
2 tablespoons soy sauce
1 teaspoon *mirin*, Japanese sweet cooking wine
1 tablespoon sugar
⅛ teaspoon salt

1. Soften *shiitake* mushrooms in 1 cup of water; trim stems. Cut into halves.

BRAISED CHICKEN WINGS

1. Mix chicken wings with 1 teaspoon grated ginger root and 1 tablespoon soy sauce; set aside.
2. Heat the wok to medium high heat; swirl in 2 tablespoons oil. Add minced garlic and ginger root; stir-fry for 30 seconds. Add chicken wings and stir-fry until golden brown.

3. Add soup stock, fish sauce, oyster sauce, sugar and pepper; bring to a boil. Cook chicken until tender.
4. Add vegetables and cook over medium heat until vegetables are tender.

5. Thicken with cornstarch mixture if you prefer.

INGREDIENTS: 4 servings

14 ounces (400g) chicken wings
1 teaspoon fresh grated ginger root
1 tablespoon soy sauce
2 tablespoons vegetable oil
2 cloves garlic, minced
1 tablespoon fresh grated ginger root
1 cup soup stock

2 tablespoons fish sauce
1 tablespoon oyster sauce
1 teaspoon sugar
Dash of pepper
½ cup chopped onion
1 tablespoon chopped green onion
3 ounces (90g) green beans cooked
(optional)

STIR-FRIED PORK CANTONESE STYLE

INGREDIENTS: 4 servings

1 pound (450g) pork, sliced thin against the grain
1 clove garlic, minced
1 tablespoon grated fresh ginger root
1 teaspoon salt
Dash of pepper
1 teaspoon sugar
1 teaspoon *sake* or cooking wine
1 tablespoon vegetable oil
½ teaspoon hot chili oil
1 onion
1 ounce (30g) pea pods or green beans, cooked
3 ounces (90g) sliced bamboo shoots
½ ounces (15g) dried cloud ears, softened
1 tablespoon soy sauce
½ cup soup stock
1 tablespoon cornstarch dissolved in 2 tablespoons water

1. Blanch pea pods. Soften dried cloud ears as shown below.

2. Heat the wok to high heat; swirl in vegetable oil; add garlic and ginger root and stir-fry for 30 seconds. Add pork and stir-fry for 5 minutes.

3. Season with salt and pepper, sugar and *sake*.

DRIED CLOUD EARS PREPARATION

4. Add onion, pea pods, bamboo shoots and cloud ears; stir-fry for 1 minute. Add soy sauce and soup stock and continue to cook for 1 to 2 minutes over medium heat.

5. Thicken with cornstarch mixture.

1. Soak in warm water to soften.

2. Trim off hard ends from softened cloud ears.

INGREDIENTS: 4 servings

2½ to 3 pounds (1⅓ to 1⅔ kg) chicken wings or broiler-fryer cut-up chicken

Teriyaki Marinade Sauce:
- 4 tablespoons soy sauce
- 1 teaspoon grated fresh ginger

1 tablespoon *sake* or cooking sherry
1 clove, garlic, crushed
1 teaspoon sugar
1 tablespoon honey
Dash of pepper
2 tablespoons vegetable oil

1. Cut chicken into serving pieces. Mix marinade sauce ingredients. Marinate chicken pieces in the sauce for 1 hour or longer.

2. Heat the wok to medium high heat; swirl in 2 tablespoons oil. Add chicken pieces and stir-fry until golden brown.

3. Add remaining marinade sauce.

4. Cook covered over medium hea until most marinade sauce i absorbed.

STIR-FRIED CHICKEN WITH OYSTER SAUCE

INGREDIENTS: 4 servings

2 pounds (900g) chicken, cut into small pieces
1 tablespoon vegetable oil
1 teaspoon sesame oil
1 teaspoon salt
2 cloves garlic, minced
1 tablespoon minced fresh ginger root

2 tablespoons oyster sauce
1 tablespoon low-salt soy sauce
1 teaspoon *sake* or cooking wine
½ cup soup stock
⅔ cup sliced mushrooms
2 tablespoons cornstarch dissolved in 2 tablespoons water

1. Cut chicken into small serving sizes.
Heat the wok to medium high heat; swirl in vegetable and sesame oil. Add salt, garlic, ginger root; stir-fry for 20 seconds.

2. Add chicken pieces; stir-fry until all sides are browned.

3. Add oyster sauce, soy sauce, *sake* and soup stock. Cover and cook for 10 minutes.

4. Add mushrooms. Thicken with cornstarch mixture.

SIMMERED SEA VEGETABLES

INGREDIENTS: 2 servings

2 ounces (60g) dried *hijiki*, a type of sea vegetation
2 slices deep-fried *tofu* pouch
1¾ ounces (50g) carrot, cut into julienne strips
2 tablespoons vegetable oil

Simmering Broth:
  ⅓ cup soup stock
  4 tablespoons low-salt soy sauce
  1 tablespoon *mirin*, Japanese sweet cooking wine
1 teaspoon toasted white sesame seeds

HIJIKI PREPARATION

1. Place dry *hijiki* in a strainer and soak in water for 30 minutes or until soft.

2. Drain water.

1. Prepare *hijiki* as shown left.

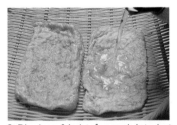

2. Dip deep-fried *tofu* pouch into hot water to remove excess oil. Pat dry with paper towels. Slice into halves lengthwise and slice into fine shreds.

3. Heat oil in the wok over medium heat; add softened *hijiki*.

4. Add deep-fried *tofu* pouch and carrot; stir well and cook for 3 to 4 minutes.

5. Mix all simmering broth ingredients and add the broth to the wok. Mix well. Cook over medium heat for 15 minutes. Sprinkle with toasted sesame seeds.

74

STEAMED CLAMS WITH BASIL THAI STYLE

INGREDIENTS: 4 servings

1 pound (450g) clams
2 tablespoons *sake* or white wine
1 teaspoon curry powder
1 teaspoon sugar
1 ½ tablespoons fish sauce
1 tablespoon minced fresh ginger root
¼ cup basil leaves
1 teaspoon cornstarch dissolved in 2 teaspoons water

1. Prepare clams as shown right.

3. Add curry powder, sugar, fish sauce and minced fresh ginger root; stir-fry for 2 to 3 minutes.

2. Place clams in the wok and pour in 2 tablespoons *sake* or wine; cover and steam for 3 minutes over high heat or shells open up.

4. Add basil leaves and cornstarch mixture; stir until thickened.

CLAM PREPARATION

1. Soak clams in salted water for several hours.

2. Wash clams under running water.

DEEP-FRYING

Deep-frying requires a large amount of oil in the wok, usually not more than 3 to 4 cups. A 14-inch (35cm) wok is best suited for deep-frying. As with stir-frying, timing and temperature for deep-frying will vary depending upon whether a gas or electric stove is used. Thus, the time given for most recipe is only approximate and adjustments should be made accordingly.

DEEP-FRYING

DEEP-FRYING OIL TEMPERATURE
Low : (300°F-320°F)
(150°C-160°C)

If the drop of batter sinks and slowly returns to the surface, the oil is not yet hot enough.

Moderate : (340°F-360°F)
(170°C-180°C)

If the batter drops to the bottom and immediately bounces up to the surface, the oil is ready for deep-frying.

High : (375°F-400°F)
(190°C-204°C)

If the drop of batter does not sink in oil or if the oil smokes, it has gotten too hot and the temperature should be lowered.

Maintain a constant frying temperature.

Added caution should be exercised whenever oil is used at high temperatures.
Drop the ingredients one at a time in the oil. Adjust the temperature to maintain a constant frying temperature.

Start with vegetables.

Start with vegetables and then shrimp or other seafood which requires a higher temperature. Skim the surface of the oil occasionally to keep it clean.

INGREDIENTS : 4 servings

4 slices white meat fish (cod, red snapper, halibut fillets)
1 tablespoon *sake* or white wine
1 egg, lightly beaten
3 tablespoons all-purpose flour
1 tablespoon ice water
Oil for deep-frying

Sweet & Sour Sauce:
1 can (8 ounces, 225g) pineapple chunks
3 tablespoons rice vinegar
3 tablespoons sugar
1 tablespoon cornstarch dissolved in 2 tablespoons water
2 tablespoons chopped Szechuan prepared vegetables or
4 tablespoons chopped sweet pickles
2 tablespoons soy sauce
2 tablespoons chopped green pepper

1. Sprinkle *sake* on fish fillets.

2. Combine egg, flour and water to make batter. Dip fish fillets in the batter.

3. Heat deep-frying oil in the wok to 340°F (170°C). Deep-fry fish fillets until golden brown. Drain and transfer onto a serving plate.

4. Combine all sweet & sour sauce ingredients and bring to a boil or until thickened. Pour over the fish.

WHOLE FISH WITH VEGETABLE SAUCE

INGREDIENTS: 2 servings

2 small whole horse mackerel or trout
Salt and pepper to taste
1 tablespoon *sake* or white wine
3 tablespoons all-purpose flour
½ teaspoon grated lemon peel
Oil for deep-frying
¼ cup shredded carrot, or julienne
strips
1 green pepper, seeded and sliced
½ onion
¼ fresh *shiitake* mushrooms, sliced
½ cup cooked bamboo shoots, cut
into julienne strips

½ clove garlic, minced
1 teaspoon grated ginger root
2 tablespoons vegetable oil
1 tablespoon sesame oil

Vegetable Sauce:

Ⓐ
⎧ 1 tablespoon soy sauce
⎪ 1 ½ tablespoons rice vinegar
⎨ 1 ½ tablespoons sugar
⎪ 1 teaspoon ketchup
⎩ ⅔ cup soup stock

½ tablespoon cornstarch dissolved in
1 tablespoon water

1. Sprinkle wine, salt pepper on fish. Prepare whole horse mackerel as shown below.

2. Combine flour and lemon peel. Coat the fish with flour mixture.

3. Heat deep-frying oil to 340°F (170°C to 180°C); deep-fry fish until golden brown on both sides. Transfer onto a rack to drain, then to a serving platter. Set aside and keep warm. Prepare all vegetables. Combine all Ⓐ ingredients and set aside.

4. Heat the wok to medium high heat; swirl in vegetable and sesame oil; stir-fry garlic and ginger root for 30 seconds. Add all vegetables and Shiitake mushrooms stir-fry for 2 minutes or until vegetables are crisp tender over high heat.

FISH PREPARATION

5. Add mixture of Ⓐ ingredients and bring to a boil. Add cornstarch mixture and combine. Cook until thickened. Pour over the fish.

1. After soaking in salted water, remove "hard scales" from tail end.

2. Insert knife under pectoral fin at right angles and cut off gill.

3. Cut off fin.

4. Make a slit in belly to anal fin.

5. Remove entrails and wash and pat dry with paper towels.

78

INGREDIENTS: 2 servings

10 ounces (300g) thin sliced
beef
2 carrot sticks, cooked
4 asparagus stalks, cooked
Batter:
- ½ cup all-purpose flour
- ½ cup ice water
- eggs, lightly beaten
- ¼ teaspoon hot bean paste
- 1 ½ tablespoons red *miso*, soy
  bean paste

Oil for deep-flying
※Boneless chicken breast can
be substituted for beef.

Garnishes:
Lemon wedges
Parsley

1. Prepare beef rolls as shown
below.

2. Make egg batter and dip rolled
beef.

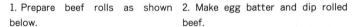

3. Heat oil to 350°F (175°C); deep-fly
rolled beef a few minutes until light
golden brown. Drain. Cut in half if
you desire.

BEEF ROLL PREPARATION

1. Place thinly sliced beef in front of
you. Place one carrot and two asparagus stalks on top. Cup off excess
carrot and asparagus.

2. Roll up.

TOFU TEMPURA

INGREDIENTS: 4 servings

2 blocks firm *tofu*, well drained
1 cup all-purpose flour
Oil for deep-frying

Tempura Sauce:
⎧ 1 ⅓ cups soup stock
⎪ 2½ tablespoons light-color
⎪ soy sauce
⎪ 1 tablespoon *mirin*, Japanese
⎩ sweet cooking wine

Garnishes:
4 tablespoons grated *daikon* radishes
4 teaspoons grated fresh ginger root
2 teaspoons minced green onion
Some bonito flakes
7-spice powder

1 Drain *tofu* well, place *tofu* on cutting board and tilt to one side, or place *tofu* between two sheets of paper towels to drain.
Cut *tofu* into eighths.

2. Coat with flour. Set aside.

3. Heat deep-frying oil to 350°F (175° C). Deep-fry *tofu* pieces until lightly browned. Drain.

4. Mix tempura sauce ingredients in a small saucepan; heat and bring to a boil.
Place fried *tofu* in an individual bowl and pour hot sauce over. Serve with garnishes.

INGREDIENTS: 4 servings
20 ounces (600g) medium oysters, drained
¼ teaspoon salt
⅛ teaspoon pepper
⅔ cup all purpose flour
2 eggs, lightly beaten
1 ⅓ cups grated fresh bread crumbs
Oil for deep-frying
1 lemon, cut into wedges
Sauce:
⎡ 6 tablespoons mayonnaise
⎜ 1 small sweet pickle, minced
⎜ 1 tablespoon chopped onion
⎜ 1 hard-boiled egg, shelled and
⎜ chopped
⎣ ½ teaspoon minced parsley

1. Wash oysters under running water and drain well.

2. Sprinkle salt and pepper. Prepare flour, beaten eggs and bread crumbs in individual containers. Coat oyster with flour, beaten eggs and bread crumbs as shown belows.

3. Heat oil in the wok to 340°F (170° C); drop 5 or 6 oysters into hot oil and deep-fry until golden brown, turning once, 2 to 3 minutes. Drain excess oil on paper towels. Repeat the same process with remaining oysters.

4. Mix all sauce ingredients and serve with deep-fried oysters. Garnish with lemon wedges.

PREPARATION OF OYSTERS

1. Coat oyster with flour, first; shake off excess flour.

2. Dip into beaten eggs.

3. Coat with bread crumbs. Press oyster; shake off excess bread crumbs.

CRISPY DEEP-FRIED SOLE

INGREDIENTS: 2 servings
2 fresh sole
4 tablespoons cornstarch or all-purpose flour
¼ teaspoon grated lemon peel
Condiments:
Grated *daikon* radish
Lemon wedges
or sweet and sour sauce

Sweet and Sour Sauce:
⅔ cup soup stock.
1 tablespoon soy sauce
1 tablespoon sugar
1 tablespoon rice vinegar
1 tablespoon ketchup
1 teaspoon cornstarch dissolved in 1 teaspoon water
Oil for deep-frying

1. Prepare sole as shown below.

2. Make one or two slit diagonally.

3. Mix cornstarch and grated lemon peel. Coat fish with cornstarch.

4. Heat deep-frying oil to 350°F (180° C). Slide head into hot oil holding tail; then deep-fry fish for a few minutes. Turn over and deep fry until light brown. Drain on paper towels. Serve hot.

5. For sweet and sour sauce, heat all sauce ingredients except cornstarch over medium high heat until sugar dissolves. Add cornstarch mixture and stir until thickened.

SOLE PREPARATION

1. Scrape off scales. Cut off pectoral fin on both sides.

2. Make a slit in belly to anal fin.

3. Remove entrails carefully with a tip of knife. Wash under running water and wipe dry.

SPRING ROLLS

INGREDIENTS: Makes 16 to 20 rolls

20 spring roll wrappers

Filling:

1 pound (450g) ground chicken
1 *shiitake* mushroom, softened and thinly sliced
1 cup beansprouts, blanched
1 green onion, chopped
4 tablespoons chopped bamboo shoots
4 tablespoons chopped celery
3 tablespoons soy sauce
1 tablespoon cooking wine or *sake*
2 tablespoons cornstarch
2 tablespoons vegetable oil
Oil for deep-frying

VEGETABLE ROLLS

INGREDIENTS: Makes 16 rolls

16 spring roll wrappers

Filling:

2 stalks celery
1 cup chopped carrot
1 clove garlic, minced
1 pound (450g) beansprouts
3 *shiitake* mushrooms, softened
½ teaspoon sesame oil
1 tablespoon soy sauce
½ teaspoon curry powder
⅛ teaspoon sugar
1 tablespoon vegetable oil

1. Slice *shiitake* mushrooms.

1. Chop celery stalks. Trim stem ends of *shiitake* mushrooms, then slice.

2. Heat a wok; swirl in 1 tablespoon oil. Add garlic; stir-fry for 20 seconds over high heat.
Add vegetables and *shiitake* mushrooms; stir-fry for 1 minute.

2. Heat the wok to medium high; swirl in 2 tablespoons oil.
Add ground chicken, *sake* and soy sauce; stir-fry for 1 minute.

3. Add sesame oil, soy sauce, curry powder and sugar.
Cook for another 1 minute.
Allow filling to cool before wrapping. Whatever the liquids is left, drain from the filling.

4. Make rolls as shown below.

3. Add all vegetables and *shiitake* mushrooms; stir-fry for 2 minutes. Add cornstarch. Toss and cook for 1 minute.

4. Allow to cool filling ingredients. Strain liquid. Filling should not drip.

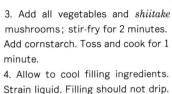

5. Heat deep-frying oil to 350°F (175°C) and deep-fry rolls for 3 minutes or until golden brown. Serve with favorite dip.

5. Heat deep frying oil to 375°F (190°C). Drop each roll in oil and deep-fry for 2 minutes or until golden brown.

SPRING ROLL PREPARATION

1. Place wrapper as shown above. Spread 2 tablespoons filling ingredients in lower portion of the wrapper.

2. Fold lower portion of corner in.

3. Then fold sides in.

4. Roll up. Moisten upper portion of wrapper with water and roll up entire roll.

PORK & ONION KABOBS

INGREDIENTS: Makes 8 kabobs
14 ounces (400g) boneless pork loin, cut into 16 chunks
2 leeks, cut into 1½-inch (4cm) lengths
8 small mild green chilies or 4 green peppers, cut into quarters
Salt and pepper and all-purpose flour for dusting
2 eggs plus 1 teaspoon water, lightly beaten
1½ to 2 cups bread crumbs
Oil for deep-frying
Garnish:
Lemon wedges

1. Sprinkle pork chunks with salt and pepper.

2. Skewer leek, pork, leek and pork as shown above. Makes 8 kabobs.

3. Coat each kabob with flour, beaten eggs and bread crumbs.

4. Prick green chili two to three places to prevent shrinking while deep-frying.

5. Heat oil to 340°F (170°C) and deep-fry 2 or 3 kabobs at a time. Turn and cook until golden brown. Drain on paper towels. Deep-fry well dried green peppers without coating.

6. Put green pepper on top or end of eack kabob. Garnish with lemon wedges.

CRISPY CHICKEN NUGGETS

INGREDIENTS: 4 to 6 servings
16 drumsticks or 2 pounds (900g) chicken wings
Marinade Sauce:
- 2 teaspoons fresh ginger juice, grated fresh ginger root
- 4 tablespoons soy sauce
- 2 tablespoons *sake*, or cooking wine
- 2 tablespoons *mirin*, Japanese sweet cooking wine

4 tablespoons cornstarch for coating
Oil for deep-frying

1. Cut drumsticks into walnut-size nuggets. Marinate the drumsticks for 30 minutes to 1 hour.

2. Wipe off excess sauce from drumsticks. Dust drumsticks with cornstarch.

VARIATION
SWEET & SOUR CHICKEN NUGGETS

INGREDIENTS: 4 to 6 servings
Crispy chicken nuggets
Sweet & Sour Sauce:
2 slices pineapple
⅔ cup mixture of pineapple juice and water
4 tablespoons sugar
3 tablespoons rice vinegar
2 tablespoons cornstarch
1 tablespoon ketchup
Garnish:
Cherry tomatoes

1. Cut pineapple into chunks. Set aside.

2. Combine all sauce ingredients and heat over medium heat until thickened. Add deep-fried chicken nuggets and combine and bring to a boil. Add pineapple chunks. Remove from heat.

3. Heat deep-frying oil to 375°F (190° C); deep-fry drumsticks for 5 minutes or until golden brown. Drain.

LOTUS ROOT TEMPURA DELIGHT

INGREDIENTS: 4 servings

7 ounces (200g) lotus root

Ⓐ
- 1 teaspoon rice vinegar
- 3 cups water
- 1 teaspoon salt

¼ pound (115g) ground chicken

Ⓑ
- 1 teaspoon soy sauce
- 1 teaspoon *sake*
- 1 teaspoon ginger juice from grated fresh ginger
- 1 egg yolk
- 2 teaspoons cornstarch

Tempura **Batter:**
- 1 egg white
- ¼ cup cornstarch dissolved in 1 table spoon chilled water
- 2 tablespoons minced parsley sprigs

Oil for deep-frying

1. Peel lotus root, slice into ½ inch (1.27cm) thick rounds. Heat Ⓐ ingredients solution to a boil; add lotus root and cook for 5 minutes. Drain and set aside.

2. Mix ground chicken and Ⓑ ingredients.

3. Stuff chicken mixture into lotus root holes with a teaspoon.

4. In a chilled bowl, lightly beaten egg white and add cornstarch mixture and parsley. Use chopsticks or fork to fold loosely.

5. Coat lotus root lightly with cornstarch.

6. Heat oil in the wok to 340°F (170 C). Dip lotus root into batter and deep-fry until golden. Drain on rack.

SEAFOOD TEMPURA

INGREDIENTS: 4 servings

12 medium prawns

2 fillets of small white meat fish (red snapper or cod)

2 green peppers

2 small eggplants

2 large *shiitake* mushrooms, softened

4 slices carrot, cut into ½-inch (1 cm) thick rounds

Some green-beans (optional)

Tempura Batter:

- 2 eggs
- 1½ cups ice water
- 2 cups sifted all purpose flour
- 1 teaspoon cornstarch
- 1 teaspoon *sake* or white cooking wine

Tempura Dipping Sauce:

- 1¾ cups soup stock
- ⅓ cup soy sauce
- ⅓ cup *mirin* Japanese sweet cooking wine
- 1 teaspoon sugar

Condiments:

Finely chopped scallion

Grated daikon radish

Chili pepper

Sesame seeds

Lemon juice or lemon wedges

Oil for deep-flying

3. Break eggs into well chilled bowl; add ice water, *sake* and sifted flour.

4. Stir and make lumpy batter. Never mix well. Loosely fold with chopsticks or fork and batter should be a mixture of dry flour for crispy tempura.

Heat oil to 330°F to 355°F (165°C to 180°C) depending on ingredients. Test oil temperature by dropping a tiny bit of batter into the oil; it should float to the surface from halfway to the bottom of the oil. Oil is then ready for deep-frying.

7. In a sauce pan, bring all tempura dipping sauce ingredients to a boil and let stand to cool.

Serve Tempura with dipping sauce and condiments of your choice.

5. Pat dry all ingredients thoroughly. Start with vegetables. Coat with lumpy batter; slide into hot oil and deep-fry until golden, turning once or twice for even cooking.

PRAWNS PREPARATION

1. Cut off heads from prawns.

2. Devein and shell as shown with a skewer, leaving tail attached.

1. Prepare prawns as shown below.

2. Cut each eggplant and green pepper lengthwise into quarters and remove seeds from green peppers. Cut *shiitake* mushrooms into quarters.

6. For prawns pinch tail with fingers; dip into batter, but leaving tail uncoated. Slide into hot oil. Drain excess oil on paper towels after deep-frying.

3. To prevent from curling while deep-frying, make a few incisions along the belly and back side.

4. To prevent oil splattering while prawns are deep-fried, chop off tips of prawn tails and gently press out water using the side of a knife tip.

5. Shell prawns.

BOILING, BLANCHING

The wok is deep, like a soup pot, so you can boil vegetables, rice and other ingredients and make soup in it. The wok is the all-purpose cooking pot.

BOILING & BLANCHING

Fill wok with water until almost ⅔ full.

Boil or blanch the vegetables in a generous amount of rapidly boiling unsalted water such as carrots.

Retain colors

Add a small amount of salt in a rapidly boiling water. Blanch broccoli or asparagus for 1 minute, then transfer to an ice water to retain the bright green color.

Parboling

You may need some special cutting techniques for vegetables such as diagonal slices flower-cuts, trimming to enhance the appearance of the finished dish.

Start from stem ends.

Blanch the vegetables such as bo choy or other Chinese greens from the stem ends, then blanch gree leaves. Transfer them to an ic water bath to chill, then drain.

SPICY & SOUR MUSHROOM SOUP

INGREDIENTS: 4 servings

- 10 medium *shiitake* mushrooms
- 1 pack *shimeji* mushrooms
- ½ cup sliced fresh button mushrooms
- ½ small onion
- 2 cloves garlic, minced
- 3 ounces (90g) chicken, deboned & skinned
- 2 tablespoons olive oil
- 4 cups water

Ⓐ {
- 5 kaffir lime leaves
- 6 tablespoons lime juice
- 6 tablespoons fish sauce
- 1 stalk lemon grass, cut into 1 inch (2.5cm) lengths using lower ⅓ portion only
- 1 tablespoon sugar
- ¼ to ½ teaspoon crushed chili pepper
}
- 4 tablespoons cilantro sprigs
- Few drops hot chili oil (optional)

1. Mince onion. Cut chicken meat into small pieces. Slice shiitake mushrooms into ¼-inch (5mm) thick. Trim stems of *shimeji* mushrooms.

MUSHROOM PREPARATION

1. Wipe off cup of mushrooms.

2. Slice them just before cooking.

2. Heat the wok to medium high, swirl in the olive oil; add garlic and stir-fry for 30 seconds. Add chicken and stir-fry for 2 to 3 minutes; add minced onion and stir-fry another 2 minutes.

3. Add shiitake, shimeji and button mushrooms and turn heat to high. Pour 4 cups water and bring to a boil. Skim froth.

4. Turn heat to medium low and add Ⓐ ingredients. Simmer for 10 minutes. Garnish soup with cilantro and hot chili oil if you desire.

INGREDIENTS: 4 servings

½ pound (225g) cocktail shrimp
¼ pound (115g) surimi, ground fresh fish fillet
1 egg white

Ⓐ ⎧ 2 tablespoons cornstarch
⎪ ½ teaspoon salt
⎪ ⅛ teaspoon grated fresh ginger root
⎪ ⅛ teaspoon crushed garlic
⎪ 1 teaspoon white wine or *sake*
⎩ ¼ teaspoon fish sauce

Soup Stock:
3 cups chicken stock
2 tablespoons minced green onion
½ teaspoon minced parsley
1½ tablespoons light-color soy sauce
Some orange or lemon peel

1. Chop cocktail shrimp into fine pieces. Mix shrimp with surimi.

2. Lightly beaten egg white; add all Ⓐ ingredients.

3. Mix with shrimp mixture. Wet palm of your hands and form shrimp balls (walnut size).

4. Heat soup stock ingredients to boild; drop shrimp balls a few pieces at a time; adjust heat to medium and skim froth during cooking the shrimp balls.

5. Serve hot and garnish with some peel.

COCONUT MILK WITH TOFU

INGREDIENTS: 4 to 6 servings

1 can (14-ounces, 400ml) coconut milk
¾ cup water
1 block firm *tofu*, well drained
3 ounces (90g) chicken breast, skinned, deboned or ground chicken
1 teaspoon *sake* or white cooking wine
5 slices fresh Thai ginger root or regular ginger root
1 tablespoon chopped lemon grass
5 dried or fresh kaffir lime leaves
3 tablespoons fish sauce
3 tablespoons lime juice
1 tablespoon sugar
⅓ cup thinly sliced fresh *shiitake* mushrooms (or ⅓ cup straw mushrooms)
⅓ cup thinly sliced button mushrooms
Dash of cayenne pepper
Tabasco (optional)
Minced parsley or cilantro (optional)

1. Cut *tofu* crosswise into halves; then cut into 1-inch (2.5cm) cubes.

2. Slice chicken breast into thin slices; sprinkle sake. Set aside.

3. In the wok, pour ¾ cup water; bring to a boil. Add lemon grass, garanga, chicken and kaffir lime leaves and bring to a boil, again. Skim froth.

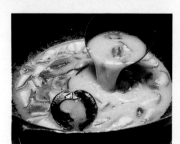

4. Add coconut milk; add fish sauce, lime juice, sugar, *shiitake* and button mushrooms just before boiling over medium high heat.

5. Add *tofu* and bring to a simmer, stirring. Remove from heat.
Remove lime leaves before serving. Sprinkle pepper and garnish with minced parsley or cilantro.

INGREDIENTS: 4 servings

1 to 1⅓ pounds (450-600g)
Chinese broccoli (or bok choy)
1 tablespoon salted black beans
3 cups water
2 tablespoons oyster sauce
2 tablespoons vegetable oil
1 teaspoon sesame oil
2 cloves garlic, minced

1. Trim off hard stem ends from Chinese broccoli. Cut into bite size.

2. Blanch Chinese broccoli in 3 cups of rapidly boiling water with 1 tablespoon salted black beans for 1 to 2 minutes. Drain and set aside.

3. Clean the wok and heat to medium high; swirl in 2 tablespoons vegetable oil and add minced garlic. Stir-fry for 30 seconds. Add oyster sauce, sesame oil and cooked chinese broccoli; combine. Serve immediately.

SHRIMP SALAD

INGREDIENTS: 4 servings
1 small head Boston or iceberg lettuce
1 green pepper
12 pea pods
½ cup shredded carrot
⅔ cup beansprouts
¼ cup sliced mushrooms
⅔ cup broccoli flowerets
½ pound (225g) shrimp
Salad Dressing:
¼ cup soy sauce
¼ cup rice vinegar
2 tablespoons sesame oil
1 tablespoon sugar
1 clove garlic, crushed
1 teaspoon grated ginger root

1. Wash and trim the lettuce. Tear it into bite-size pieces. Snap off the pea pod stems and pull back the string for the entire length of the pod. Cut the top off the green pepper and cut in half. Discard top and seeds. Slice it thin lengthwise.

2. Blanch the vegetables except lettuce one at a time in a generous amount of rapidly boiling unsalted water. As each vegetable is blanched, transfer to an ice water bath to chill, then drain.

3. Shell and devein shrimp; cook for 1 minute in a generous amount of rapidly boiling unsalted water. Drain and let it cool.

4. Combine all salad dressing ingredients. Mix all vegetables with shrimp and serve with dressing.

95

INGREDIENTS

Some of the necessary ingredients used in our recipes, however, may be unfamiliar to you.
There are listed on page 96~99 and are available at most Oriental food markets, and some health food stores and supermarkets.
The greatest assets in wok cooking are your resoucefulness, ingenuity, and ability to adapt in the face of unavailable ingredients.

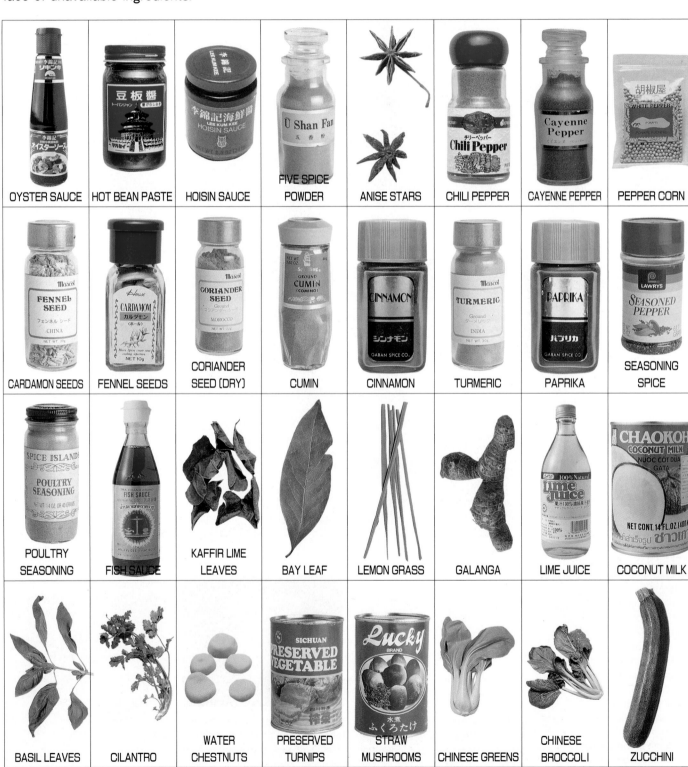

OYSTER SAUCE	HOT BEAN PASTE	HOISIN SAUCE	FIVE SPICE POWDER
ANISE STARS	CHILI PEPPER	CAYENNE PEPPER	PEPPER CORN
CARDAMON SEEDS	FENNEL SEEDS	CORIANDER SEED (DRY)	CUMIN
CINNAMON	TURMERIC	PAPRIKA	SEASONING SPICE
POULTRY SEASONING	FISH SAUCE	KAFFIR LIME LEAVES	BAY LEAF
LEMON GRASS	GALANGA	LIME JUICE	COCONUT MILK
BASIL LEAVES	CILANTRO	WATER CHESTNUTS	PRESERVED TURNIPS
STRAW MUSHROOMS	CHINESE GREENS	CHINESE BROCCOLI	ZUCCHINI

INGREDIENTS

ANISE STAR —— Brown, star-shaped seed with the taste of licorice. Keeps indefinitely.

ATSUAGE (DEEP-FRIED *TOFU* CUTLET) • *ABURA-AGE* (DEEP-FRIED *TOFU* POUCH) —— *Atsuage* is a deep-fried regular *tofu*. It is fried until the outside becomes crisp and golden brown but the inside is still white. *Abura-age* is also deep-fried *tofu* but before frying it is cut into thin sheets.

BAMBOO SHOOT —— The cone shaped shoots of the bamboo plant. It is easy to purchase the canned variety which comes whole or slices or shreds. Once opened, bamboo shoots should be stored in a different container with fresh water in the refrigerator. Change the water once every 4 to 5 days. Available at Asian grocery stores.

BABY CORN —— Small immature corn. Once opened, store in a water filled container with lid. Keeps for several days when refrigerated.

BASIL LEAF —— A fresh sweet basil with dark green leaves with a purple stem. The flavor is that of aromatic licorice. Fresh mint can be an acceptable substitute in cooking.

BAY LEAF —— An aromatic leaf with green in color. Wonderful flavoring for roast pork, beef soup and stews.

BEAN PASTE, HOT (CHILI PASTE WITH SOYBEAN) —— Soybean sauce made from soybeans, chili peppers and sometimes garlic. Comes in cans or jars. Refrigerated, it keeps indefinitely in tightly sealed jars. Degree of hotness may vary between different brands. Brown soybean sauce combined with a hot sauce can be used as a substitute.

BEAN THREADS (CELLOPHANE NOODLES) —— These are long, dry noodles made of mung bean flour. They keep on the shelf indefinitely. Soak them in warm water for 15 minutes before use. They may also be deep-fried in hot oil. Do not soak them in water prior to deep-frying. Use them as a noodle in soups, or with stir-fried vegetables and meat. To keep them as clean as possible place them in a large paper bag before removing the wrapper. Break off the amount needed and store the remainder in a bag.

BEAN SPROUTS —— Sprouts of the mung bean; about 2-in. (5 cm) long. Refrigerate sprouts covered with water. Keeps for one week. Change the water every 3 days.

BLACK BEANS, FERMENTED —— Salted, fermented, soft black bean seed. Mainly used to flavor sauces. Rinse with water before using. Keeps in a covered container on the shelf indefinitely.

CARDAMON SEED —— Native to south India and Sri Lanka. Cardamon is a prominent seasoning in Indian cooking. The whole cardamon seeds into curries and rice and remove them after cooking.

CAYENNE PEPPER —— Cayenne pepper is commonly called chilies or red pepper which is the ground product of the dried ripe fruit of several different species of small fruited Capsicum plants.

CHILI —— The small green chili is the most popular chili used in Thai cooking (known as prig kee noo). This chili is very hot and the amount used in each recipe is determined by individual preference. Other less hot varieties can be substituted. Chilies can be made less hot by removing the seeds.

CHILI PEPPER —— Dried chilies are grounded into fine powder.

CHINESE BROCCOLI —— A tender, green, seasonal vegetable available in spring and summer months. Chinese broccoli is more slender and leafy than regular broccoli. For recipes in this book, substitute with bok choy, spinach or regular broccoli cut into long slender pieces.

CHINESE GREEN —— Also called bok choy. These greens are long like romaine lettuce. Discard the tough bottom. Serve in stir-fried or steamed as cabbage.

CILANTRO —— The leafy green parsley plant often referred to as Chinese parsley, coriander is the seeds and cilantro is the leaf portion. An essential ingredient in Thai and chinese cooking.

CINNAMON —— Pungent and sweet cinnamon is available in whole and ground form. They are used for cookies, cakes, puddings, pies, fruit desserts and pickling.

CLOUD EARS —— Brown, irregular, leafy shaped fungus or mushroom with a delicate taste. Soak 15 minutes in warm water to soften. Rinse before using. Keeps indefinitely on the shelf.

COCONUT MILK —— Coconut milk is made by grating the meat of the mature fresh coconut and combining it with hot water and squeezing through a filter to extract the liquid. The resulting liquid is the coconut milk most preferred for cooking. A second repeated process results in a thinner coconut milk used mainly for cooking other recipes requiring less coconut flavor. The clear liquid in the center of a young coconut is referred to as coconut water and is usually not used in cooking but used just for drinking. Coconut milk can be purchased in cans.

CORIANDER SEED (DRY) —— Available as small brown seeds. An essential ingredient in Thai cuisine. Each portion of the parsley plant has a very distinctive flavor and use.

CUMIN —— An essential spice powder used in the making of some Thai curries and chicken or beef dish. If using seeds, roast before grinding this imparts a fuller flavor.

CURRY PASTE —— The curry blends are used in making the various curry.

DAIKON **RADISH** —— *Daikon* radish is rich in vitamins, and its leaves contain a lot of vitamin C. This radish is thought to aid digestion of oily foods. It is good for simmered dishes.

DRIED BONITO —— This is an important ingredient in *dashi* stock. A stick of dried bonito looks like a 6-8 in. (15-20cm) long brownish hunk of wood. Shaved, dried bonito flakes are also available in packs and convenient to use. Dried bonito "thread" shavings are often used as a garnish. Such "thread" shavings look like rosy-beige excelsior and has a pleasant flavor. If you cannot obtain them, use regular dried bonito flakes.

EGGPLANT —— Japanese eggplant is on the average 4 in. (10cm) long and weigh 2-3 oz (60-90g) each. Because size varies with region and season, weights are included to offer a guideline. Eggplants used here are the 6-inch (15cm) variety that weigh approximately 10 oz (285g) each.

EGG ROLL WRAPPER —— Pastry wrappers for spring rolls. Usually comes in 1 pound (450g) packages. Sold in produce or frozen food sections of supermarkets and in Oriental markets. Fresh egg roll wrappers will keep for one week in the refrigerator. Can be kept frozen for about 3 months. To thaw, unwrap the package and defrost for about one hour under a damp cloth.

ENOKITAKE **MUSHROOM** —— *Enokitake* mushroom is mild-flavored and with a pleasant crisp aroma. It is often used in soups. There are canned enokitake mushrooms but fresh is better.

FENNEL SEED —— The whole fennel seed is a light chartreuse color, but a light brown when ground. Fennel seed has a sweet, aromatic taste and the flavor resembles licorice or anise.

FISH SAUCE —— Fish sauce is made by aging salted fish in large stone jars and filtering off the liquid. It is indispensable to Thai cooking. This condiment is also used for Vietnamese, Philippine and Burmese cooking.

FIVE SPICE POWDER —— A blend of five ground spices: Szechwan peppercorns, star anise, cinnamon, fennel and cloves. Keeps on the shelf for several months.

GALANGA —— A rhizome similar in appearance to ginger root. It has a different flavor and is generally sliced. Available fresh, dried or in powdered dried form.

GARLIC —— An important ingredient in Oriental cooking. Always use fresh garlic, not powder.

GEODUCK —— This is known as horse clam and is yellowish white in color. It has an elastic type texture. It's best eaten very fresh.

GINGER ROOT —— A rhizome of the ginger plant. Young ginger has a very translucent skin, the mature ginger has a brown skin which should be peeled before using. Ginger imparts hotness and flavor to the food.

HIJIKI **(BLACK SEA VEGETABLE)** —— Dried *hijiki* is a black and brittle vegetable rich in calcuim. Soaking makes *hijiki* a tender and lustrous vegetable.

HOISIN SAUCE —— A pungent, sweet condiment sauce made of soy beans, spices, chili and sugar. Once opened, store in a jar with a tight lid. Keeps refrigerated for about 6 months.

HOT BEAN PASTE (CHILI PASTE WITH SOY BEANS) —— Soy bean sauces made from soy beans, chili peppers and sometimes garlic. It comes in cans or jars. Refrigerated, keeps indifinitely in tightly sealed jars. Degree of hotness may vary between different brands.

JAPANESE CUCUMBER —— Recipes in this book call for American cucumbers, which are equivalent to 2 or 3 Japanese cucumbers. In general, peel and seed cucumbers unless the skin is delicate and the thin and seeds are immature. If using the Japanese variety, it is not necessary to peel or seed. However to smooth the rough surface and to bring out the skin color, dredge the cucumber in salt and roll it back and forth on a cutting board using the palm of your hand. Wash well.

JAPANESE HOT PEPPER —— Red pepper is used fresh or dried. Dried and ground coarse pepper is called *ichimi*, or one flavor spice. This ichimi is one of the component ingredients of *shichimi* or 7-spice mixture. *Shichimi* is a collection of seven dried and ground flavors: red pepper flakes (*togarashi*); roughly ground, brown *sansho* pepper pods; minute flakes of dried mandarin orange peel; dark green *nori* seaweed bits; black kemp seeds; white poppy seeds; and black sesame seeds.

KAFFIR LIME —— This lime has a bumpy outer skin and only the skin is used. The juice of this lime is seldom used in cooking.

KOMBU **(KELP)** —— *Kombu* is one of one of the basic ingredients used for making *dashi* stock. When you use it, never wash or rinse. The speckled surface of the kelp holds flavor, so do not wash. Kelp contains the most iodine of all seaweeds.

LEMON GRASS —— A tall, strong, graceful grass found in Thailand and other warm weather countries. The plant has a tough fibrous stem with a very delicate refreshing aroma resembling that of lemons.

LIME —— Thai limes are smaller, stronger and much juicier than other limes. Fresh lime juice is preferred for all recipes.

LIME JUICE —— It is made of juice from squeezed fresh lime.

LIME LEAF —— The leaf of the kaffir lime plant. The leaf imparts a delicate fresh distinctive flavor to the dish. No substitution. Fresh kaffir lime leaf is preferred but dried kaffir lime leaf may be used.

LOTUS ROOT —— The flesh is white and "crunchy". Long tubular hollows run through the entire length of the root. When preparing lotus root for cooking, pare it first. Then cut into rounds. The shape should be attractive. To prevent discoloring it should be immersed for a short time in a mixture of alum and water or vinegar and water. This also gets rid of any harshness in flavor. It can then be boiled in water containing a little vinegar. It goes well with vinegared dishes.

MAGGIE SAUCE —— The extract of fermented soybeans with salt and some spices. It is different in flavor from soy sauce. Generally it is used for Thai cooking.

MASAMAN CURRY PASTE —— A blend of dried red chilles, onions, coriander and other spices and herbs.

MINT LEAF —— The fresh leaves of mint. Used in recipes to impart refreshing aroma.

MIRIN —— *Mirin* is heavily sweetened *sake*, used for cooking. *Mirin* is called "sweet cooking rice wine". *Sake* sweetened with sugar can be substituted.

MISO —— *Miso* is fermented soybean paste. The colors range from yellow to brown; yellow *miso* is referred to as white *miso* in this book. Brown *miso* is called red *miso*. Since there are various kinds of *miso*, it might be helpful to learn about *miso* by buying small quantities of various kinds. It is used for soups, dressings, sauces, etc...

MUSSLE —— An oval shaped shell with black color. Softer in texture than other shell fish, it is pink-orange in color. The taste is delicate and slightly sweet.

OYSTER SAUCE —— A thick brown sauce made from oysters and soy sauce. It keeps indefinitely in the refrigerator.

PANKO (DEHYDRATED BREAD CRUMBS) —— Japanese dehydrated bread crumbs with a coarse texture. Regular bread crumbs are available at most supermarkets or Oriental groceries.

PAPRIKA —— Ground paprika has slightly bitter taste. Adds color to the dishes.

PARSLEY, CHINESE (CORIANDER OR CILANTRO) —— A leafy parsley with a pungent flavor. Use as a garnish. Also may be used to add flavor to most any dish.

PEANUTS —— Fresh peanut are shelled and then blanched to remove the skin. Roast it in the oven at 350°F (175°C) until golden brown. Use as directed in the recipe. Peanut can be ground using a blender or food processor which only requires a few seconds. Grind to a coarse stage or it will turn into peanut butter. Use in cooking or in the making of peanut sauce.

PEPPERCORN (DRIED BLACK) —— Dried seed of the pepper plant. The seeds are usually ground before using. Grind just before using for freshest flavor.

(DRIED WHITE) —— The inner seed of the peppercorn. It is usually sold in ground form. It imparts a different flavor from black pepper.

POULTRY SEASONING —— It is a blend of salt, sage, onion, thyme, marjoram and other herbs. It is used for chicken, turkey, goose, duck and stuffing.

PRESERVED TURNIP —— Sliced turnips preserved in salt. Sold in most Asian groceries. Rinse off salt before using.

RED CURRY PASTE —— A blend of chilli peppers, garlic, lemon grass, cilantro, galanga and onions.

RICE (GLUTINOUS RICE) —— Stickly rice is also called sweet rice. It is often used in the making of desserts. There are many varieties of sweet rice. Some are steamed and served as the staple of a meal.

RICE NOODLE —— Noodles made from ground rice flour. These noodles come in various forms from dried to fresh. Some resemble sheets which are steamed in layers and sold fresh. Some noodles are sold dried they come in different thickness and length. Dried rice noodles must be soaked in water before cooking.

RICE VINEGAR —— Japanese rice vinegar is milder than Western vinegars. Lightness and relative sweetness are characteristic of rice vinegar. Use cider vinegar if substituting.

SAKE —— *Sake* is made by binoculating steamed mold (*koji*) and then allowing fermentation to occur. It is then refined. In Japan *sake* is the most popular beverage but it is also used in various ways in cooking.

SESAME OIL —— Made from sesame seed which is rich in oil and protein. This oil has a slightly nutty flavor that enhances sauces, salads, and seafoods. The aromatic oil can be stored in the refrigerator after opening.

SESAME SEED —— Both black and white sesame seed is used in Japanese cooking. When toasted, sesame seed has a much richer flavor. Still richer, however, is ground sesame seed. To grind sesame seed uses a *suribachi* (Japanese grinding bowl). Before grinding, toast the seeds in a dry frying pan. It is a nice garnish.

SHICHIMI-TOGARASHI (7-SPICE POWDER) —— This is a good spice for sprinkling over dishes. Because it loses its aroma quickly, buy it in small quantities and store, tightly covered.

SHIITAKE MUSHROOM —— Both fresh and dried *shiitake* mushroom can be obtained. Dried ones should be soaked in water before using. This soaking water makes *dashi* stock (Japanese soup stock). Fresh *shiitake* mushroom have a distincive, appealing "woody-fruity" flavor. *Shiitake* mushroom is good for simmered dishes because of its special flavor. The best ones have a thick, brown velvet cap and firm flesh.

SHIMEJI MUSHROOM —— Fresh *shimeji* mushrooms should be delicately crisp. The stems should be short and plump, and the flesh should be white. White mushrooms will do as a substitute if the *shimeji* mushroom are not available.

SHISO LEAF —— This minty, aromatic leaf comes in green and red varieties. The red type is to make *umeboshi* (pickled plum).

SHRIMP PASTE —— A very thick dried paste made from salty shrimp. It has a very pungent strong flavor but becomes more mellow when cooked. Stores indefinitely in a tightly sealed jar.

SOY BEAN —— Soy bean was one of the "five sacred grains" of ancient China. It's varieties include black and has yellow ones and countless uses: It can be used in stews, turned into paste, soymilk, also *tofu*, which can be used as a meat substitute.

SOY SAUCE —— Soy sauce is made from soy beans and salt. It is the primary seasoning in Japanese cooking. It is used for simmered foods, dressings, soups and; many kinds of Japanese dishes. Ordinary soy sauce is dark, but one which has a light color is also available. The light soy sauce does not darken the colors of food, and it is salty enough. Thick soy sauce is a good seasoning for raw fish, *sashimi*. It is rather sweet. Also, low-salt soy sauce is available.

SNOW PEAS (CHINESE PEA PODS) —— Flat edible pea pod. Has a delicate taste and comes fresh or frozen.

STRAW MUSHROOMS —— Small mushrooms with a round cap. Usually it comes in a can.

SZECHWAN PEPPERCORNS —— The dried berries of the prickly ash. It is not hot but has a slow numbing effect. Toast lightly in a frying pan; finely crush to a powder. Strain through a fine mesh strainer to filter the coarse shell.

TURMERIC —— Resembles ginger root in appearance but not in flavor. Turmeric has a mild, clean yet a peculiarly bitter flavor.

TOFU —— *Tofu*, "bean curd" in English, is an important product of soy beans. It is rich in protein, vitamins, calcium, and minerals. It is low in calories and saturated fats, and entirely free of cholesterol. There are two kinds of *tofu*; firm *tofu* and soft *tofu*. It is usually square shaped and creamy textured. This bland curd is made from soybeans. It also comes deep-fried and canned. Fresh bean curd, covered with water, can be kept in the refrigerator for approximately one week. Remove from the original package and replace with fresh water as soon as possible. Change the water every 2 days to keep it fresh.

TREFOIL (*MITSUBA*) —— Trefoil is a member of the parsley family. The flavor is somewhere between sorrel and celery. It accents the flavor of many Japanese dishes.

VEGETABLE OIL —— Corn oil is the first choice for the stir-frying. It is lighter. Peanut oil and safflower oil is the second best.

WATER CHESTNUT —— A walnut sized, brown bulb. It must be peeled before use. It is sweet and has a crisp texture similar to apples. Canned water chestnut is peeled and boiled. They will keep covered with fresh water, in the refrigerator, for about 2 weeks. Change the water once a week.

WINE, SHAOSING OR RICE —— Chinese rice wine used for drinking or cooking. Dry sherry may be used as a substitute in cooking.

WON TON (SUIMAI) —— Fresh squares of noodle dough. Usually comes in one pound packages. Thickness varies from thick to thin. Fresh won tons will keep in the refrigerator for one week. Can be frozen, wrapped air tight, for about 2 months. Use thick wrappers for deep-fried won tons. Thin wrappers are better for soups.

ZUCCHINI —— The size of zucchini is similar to Japanese cucumber. Cut to the appropriate size and use as directed in the recipes.

PREPARATION

HOW TO SELECT AND STORE VEGETABLE OIL

The use of polyunsaturated vegetable oil is strongly recommended for cooking. None of the pure vegetable oils contains cholesterol. Good sesame oil has a slightly nutty flavor. Store in the refrigerator after opening.

Peanut oil or good vegetable oil such as corn oil will have a longer life and possess qualities superior to other oils for deep-frying.

The used oil can be saved and used again. To grant your oil longer life, remove food crumbs with a fine mesh strainer during deep-frying. The quality of used oil is judged by its clarity, not by the number of times used nor the length of time used. Fresh oil is light yellow in color and clear. If the used oil is still relatively clear, it is salvageable and readily usable again. For the second time around, it is recommended to deep-fry chicken or meat coated with bread crumbs. To remove odour in oil, deep-fry some potatoes uncoated. The moisture in potatoes absorbs odour while it is deep-fried. The proportion of 3:1 (used oil: fresh oil) may be used for deep-frying meat and chicken, but not for *Tempura*, (deep-fried seafood Japanese style). Used oil which appears darker and clouded should be discarded because the temperature at which it will begin to smoke will drop and consequently, a high enough temperature cannot be achieved for proper deep-frying resulting in foods turning out very greasy.

HOW TO SELECT AND STORE VEGETABLES

Leafy vegetables: Look for crisp, tender leaves, free from decay. All leafier vegetables should be stored in a plastic bags and should be refrigerated.

Root vegetables: Look for firm, smooth vegetables with no ridges, blemishes or soft spots. Refrigerate onions, beets and radishes in plastic bags.

Other vegetables can be refrigerate in a crisper in plastic bags.

HOW TO SELECT AND STORE FISH

Fresh fish that is eaten raw as *sashimi* and *sushi*, must be prepared from fish that has not been out of the water for more than 24 hours. It must be properly chilled. Most fish have a shelf life of about five days. Of course the ideal fish is that which you catch yourself.

When buying fish, a reliable fish market can often provide fish of better quality than that found packaged in a supermarket. When buying fish for *sashimi* or *sushi* ask the fishmonger to cut the fish into slices, cubes, whatever you want.

If you are in doubt about the freshness of fish, do not eat it raw. Cook it according to personal preference or marinate it in *teriyaki* sauce and broil. No fresh water fish are eaten raw in *sushi* because of the possible presence of parasites. It's similar to eating pork which hasn't been cooked properly. The following are ways to check fish for freshness.

FRESH FISH

1. A mild characteristic odor, but not too strong or "fishy".
2. Bright, full, clear eyes, not milky or sunken.
3. Bright red gills, not muddy gray, free from slime.
4. Bright characteristic sheen on scales.
5. The scales which are adhering tightly to body, unblemished, without any reddish patches along the ventral area.
6. Firm or rigid body when pressed with fingers.
7. Elastic, firm flesh that does not separate easily from the bones or doesn't indent when handled.
8. Freshly cut appearance with no "leathery" traces of yellowing, browning or drying visible in the flesh.
9. Fresh fish tastes sweet and often has a cucumber-like odor.

FROZEN FISH

1. A solidly frozen package which is tightly wrapped with little or no air space between the fish and the wrapping. It should be moisture and vapour-proofed.
2. Should be kept at a storage temperature below-10°F (−23°C) in the retail food cabinet.
3. There should be no discoloration, fading or drying out in evidence.

STORING FISH

1. Since shellfish and fish are the most perishable foods, they should be used as soon as possible.
2. Wash the fish in cold, slightly salty water. Make sure to wash the stomach cavity well. Remove excess moisture with paper towels. Then wrap in waxed paper or freezer wrap. Place in the refrigerator. Handle the fish as little as possible.
3. Frozen fish should be kept frozen solid in freezer wrap or in a suitable container. Do not thaw frozen fish at room temperature before cooking, except when necessary for ease in handling. Thawing frozen fish is best achieved at refrigerator temperature. Once the fish has been thawed out, cook it immediately. Never refreeze fish that has been thawed out. It is advisable not to keep fish frozen for more than three months.

   To remove the odor from utensils, use a solution of baking soda and water. (about 1 tsp. soda to a quart of water).

   To get rid of "fishy" odors on the hands or chopping board, rub with lemon juice or sliced lemon, vinegar or salt before washing and rinse well.

A small amount of tooth paste rubbed on the hands and rinsed off is also a good deodorizer. Wine, vinegar, lemon, onion, garlic, in the recipe help to minimize the odor from cooked fish.

HOW TO SELECT RICE

There are two types of rice available: white short-grain rice and white long-grain rice. Use white short-grain rice for Japanese dishes. Long grain rice may be used for fried-rice. The short-grain rice is more glutinous than the long-grain rice. In the U.S., short-grain rice is grown extensively in California. Newly cropped rice needs less water and slightly shorter cooking time than old rice. A little practice is needed to make perfect rice, however if you cook a lot of rice, an automatic rice cooker will make your work a lot easier, so it's a good investment. Rice increases in volume as it cooks, twice to three times, depending on the kind of rice you use. The following is a key to shiny and fluffy rice. Go ahead with these basic tips for successful rice cooking. It's easy.

HOW TO COOK RICE

1. Measure rice carefully.
2. Wash the rice in a big bowl of water. Rub the grains gently since wet grains break easily.
3. Remove any bran or polishing agent. Drain off water well. Repeat this step until the water is almost clear.
4. To make fluffy and moist rice, set rice aside for at least 30 minutes in summer and one hour in winter. This allows ample time for rice to absorb water.
5. In a cooking pot, add rice and the correct amount of water. Cover with a lid.
6. Cook rice over medium heat until the water boils. Do not bring it to the boiling point quickly. If the quantity of rice is large, cook the rice over high heat from the beginning. The heat can be carried into the center of the rice if cooked over medium heat.
7. When it begins to boil, turn heat to high and cook for 1 minute. Never lift the lid while cooking. Since the lid might bounce from the pressure of the steam, it is better to place a weight, or some dished on the lid. Rice absorbs lot of water.
8. Turn the heat to low and cook for 4-5 min (Be careful not to overboil).
9. Reduce the heat to the lowest for 10 minutes. Every grain of rice absorbs water and becomes plump. It is liable to burn, so cook over the lowest heat.
10. Turn off the heat and let the rice stand, covered for 10 minutes. During this 10 minutes the grains are allowed to "settle", and the cooking process is completed by the heat retained in the rice and the walls of the pot.

UTENSILS

KNIVES

All-purpose knife
(Made of stainless steel)
Kitchen cleaver (deba-bōchō)
(Made of carbon steel)
This is used for fish, meat and poultry with bones.
Sashimi slicer (tako-biki)
(Made of carbon steel)
This is used for slicing fish fillets.
Sashimi slicer (yanagi-ba) "Willow-leaf" slicer
(Made of carbon steel)

Vegetable knife (usuba-bōchō)
(Made of carbon steel)
Paring knife
(Made of stainless steel)
Kitchen scissors
(Made of stainless steel)
Frozon food knife
(Made of stainless steel)

KNIFE SHARPENING STONE AND KNIFE SHARPENER

Knives made of carbon steel should be sharpened with stone. Always wash in hot water and wipe dry with a cloth after using. Moisten the stone with water, placing a wet cloth or kitchen towel under the stone to secure it. Place the beveled cutting edge of the blade flat on the stone. Push the blade away from you to the edge of the stone. Bring it back to the starting point and repeat this stroke with some pressure for 10-20 times and 2-3 times on the other side. All purpose knives should be sharpened with same number of strokes on both sides. Keep your knives sharp.

The beveled cutting edges

correct   wrong   wrong

BASIC CUTTING METHODS

When preparing ingredients use a sharp knife. Cut to bite size pieces making them easy to cook and to eat.
For decorative cuts, use the tip of the knife. For peeling, use the lower part of the blade.
The part from the center towards the tip is used for most cutting techniques.

Rounds	Diagonal Slices	Quarter Rounds

Round ingredients such as radish or carrot are cut into the same thickness.	Thin round ingredients such as cucumber are sliced diagonally giving a large surface.	Large round ingredients such as turnip or *daikon* radish are split into quarters and then sliced.

Half-rounds	Wedges	Rolling Wedges
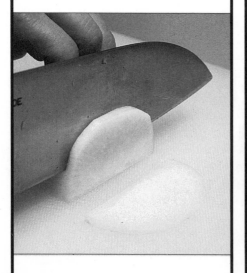		
Large round ingredients such as radish are split into halves and sliced.	Ingredients such as lemon or onion are split into quarters then eighths.	Ingredients are rolled and cut diagonally to give more sides for seasoning.

Shreds

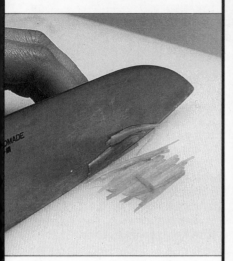

Ingredients are sliced into thin rectangles of 2-2½-inch (5-6.5cm) length, layered and cut into thin match-like sticks parallel to the fibers.

Dices

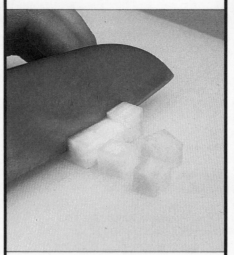

Ingredients are cut into ⅜ inch (1cm) wide sticks, and then into ⅜ inch (1cm) cubes.

Mincing

Shredded ingredients such as ginger root or green onion are chopped finely.

Cut into large pieces

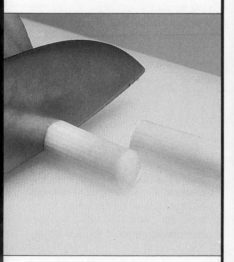

Ingredients are cut into large pieces.

Chopping

Ingredients are cut into serving pieces.

Cut into Paper Thin

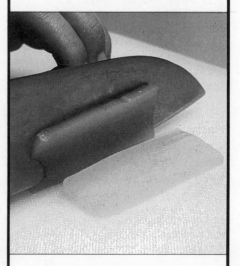

Ingredients are sliced into thin pieces.

INDEX

A
ACKNOWLEDGEMENTS ··············3
ASSORTED-MUSHROOMS SAUTÉ
  ASIAN FLAVOR ··············33

B
BASIC CUTTING METHODS 102 · 103
BEEF CURRY ··············40 · 41
BOILING, BLANCHING ··············90
BRAISED CHICKEN WINGS··············70
BRAISED GINGER PORK ··············45
BRAISED PRAWNS SZECHWAN STYLE
  ··············21
BRAISED SHIITAKE MUSHROOMS &
  BABY CORN ··············70

C
CHICKEN SIU MAI ··············52
CHICKEN TERIYAKI ··············72
CHICKEN WINGS WITH MUSHROOMS
  ··············35
CHINESE BROCCOLI WITH OYSTER
  SAUCE ··············94
CHINESE GREENS WITH CREAMY
  SAUCE ··············69
CHINESE GREENS WITH SCRAMBLED
  EGGS ··············18
COCONUT MILK WITH *TOFU* ··············93
CONTENTS ··············6~7
CRISPY CHICKEN NUGGETS ··············87
CRISPY DEEP-FRIED SOLE ··············83
CURRY FLAVORED POTATOES ··············37

D
DEEP-FRIED BEEF ROLLS ··············80
DEEP-FRIED FISH WITH SWEET &
  SOUR SAUCE ··············77
DEEP-FRIED OYSTERS JAPANESE
  STYLE ··············82
DEEP-FRIED WON TON WITH SWEET &
  SOUR SAUCE ··············43
DEEP-FRYING ··············76

E
EGG FU YUNG··············14

F
FRID RICE ··············16~17

G
GETTING TO KNOW YOUR WOK ··············9
GOLDEN OMELET··············44
GRILLED FISH FILLETS MALAYSIAN
  ··············49
GRILLED TERIYAKI FISH ··············48

H
HOISIN SAUCE PORK ··············68

I
INDEX ··············104
INGREDIENTS ··············96~99
INTRODUCTION ··············4

L
LOTUS ROOT *TEMPURA* DELIGHT
  ··············88

M
MASAMAN(MUSLIM) CURRY PASTE
  ··············40~41
MEATBALLS WITH SWEET & SOUR
  SAUCE ··············61
MEATLOAF ··············64
MENU PLANNING & BEFORE YOU
  BEGIN··············5
METRIC TABLES · BASIC COOKING
  INFORMATION ··············8

O
ORANGE BEEF WITH BROCCOLI ···42

P
PORK & ONION KABOBS ··············86
PORK POT STICKERS ··············43
PREPARATIONS ··············100~101

R
RED CURRY PASTE ··············40~41

S
SAUTÉED LEMON FLAVORED
  SARDINES ··············46~47
SAUTÉED LIVERS AND GARIC
  STALKS ··············31
SEAFOOD FRIED RICE ··············16 · 17
SEAFOOD *TEMPURA* ··············89
SEASONING YOUR WOK ··············11
SHRIMP & VEGETABLES WITH
  EXOTIC SAUCE ··············28
SHRIMP BALL SOUP ··············92
SHRIMP SALAD ··············95
SHRIMP WITH VEGETABLES ··············13
SIMMERED SEA VEGETABLES ··············74
SIMMERING, BRAISING··············66
SPICED BEEF & NUTS ··············38
SPICY & SOUR MUSHROOM SOUP···91
SPICY STEAMED EGGPLANT ··············53
SPICY *TOFU* SZECHUAN STYLE ···20
SPRING ROLLS ··············84~85
STEAMED CHICKEN & *TOFU* LOAF
  ··············58
STEAMED CHICKEN BREAST
  CHINESE STYLE ··············63
STEAMED CLAMS WITH BASIL THAI
  STYLE ··············75
STEAMED CODFISH ··············56
STEAMED EGG CUSTARD··············55

STEAMED FISH ··············59
STEAMED LAYERED CABBAGE &
  GROUND CHICKEN ··············51
STEAMED MUSSELS WITH CILANTRO
  ··············60
STEAMED PORK WITH VEGETABLES
  ··············65
STEAMED TURNIPS, JAPANESE
  STYLE ··············62
STEAMED WHOLE FISH CHINESE
  STYLE ··············54
STEAMING··············50
STIR-FRIED CHICKEN WITH OYSTER
  SAUCE ··············73
STIR-FRIED CHINESE NOODLES WITH
  VEGETABLES ··············36
STIR-FRIED CRABMEAT WITH *TOFU*
  ··············26
STIR-FRIED GEODUCK ··············24~25
STIR-FRIED GROUND MEAT &
  EGGPLANT ··············29
STIR-FRIED LETTUCE··············27
STIR-FRIED PORK CANTONESE
  STYLE ··············71
STIR-FRIED SHRIMP THAI STYLE ···32
STIR-FRIED SNOW PEAS &
  MUSHROOMS ··············22
STIR-FRIED SPICY PORK ··············19
STIR-FRIED THAI BEEF ··············23
STIR-FRIED THICK NOODLES ··············48
STIR-FRYING, SAUTÉING ··············12
SWEET & SOUR CHICKEN NUGGETS
  ··············87
SWEET & SOUR PORK ··············15

T
THAI NOODLES ··············39
TOFU TEMPURA··············81
TOFU & VEGETABLES IN MISO
  SAUCE ··············34
TWICE COOKED PRAWN DELIGHT ···67
TWICE STEAMED SWEET RICE, *ZEN*
  STYLE ··············57

U
UTENSILS ··············10 · 101

V
VEGETABLE CURRY ··············40~41
VEGETABLE ROLLS ··············84~85
VEGETABLES WITH FIVE-SPICE
  POWDER ··············30
VEGETARIAN DELIGHT SALAD ··············62

W
WHOLE FISH WITH VEGETABLE
  SAUCE ··············78~79